Famous Problems and Their Mathematicians

Art Johnson

1999
TEACHER IDEAS PRESS
A Division of
Libraries Unlimited, Inc.
Englewood, Colorado

For my loving wife, Juanita,
who has been my companion and complement in everything.

TEACHER IDEAS PRESS
A Division of
Libraries Unlimited, Inc.
P.O. Box 6633
Englewood, CO 80155-6633
1-800-237-6124
www.lu.com/tip

Library of Congress Cataloging-in-Publication Data

Johnson, Art, 1946–
    Famous problems and their mathematicians / Art Johnson.
        p. cm.
    Includes index.
    ISBN 1-56308-446-5 (pbk.)
    1. Mathematics--Problems, exercises, etc.   2. Mathematics--History.   I. Title.
    QA43.J56   1998
    510'.76--dc21   98-41449
                                                        CIP

Contents

Introduction

Many students view mathematics as a necessary discipline, but a discipline devoid of human interest with little relevance to the present or society. The reasons for this are many. Mathematics has its own language and code, which many students never master, so it appears to have the trappings of a cult. Mathematics appears fully formed, with no sense of the trial and error or progressive developments that are integral to all other disciplines. Mathematics appears to be static because there are few developments within the discipline that most students can comprehend. Finally, many students find it difficult to identify with mathematicians. If a student can name a mathematician, it is likely to be an ancient Greek, rather than a modern practitioner. This state of affairs is lamentable because mathematics, perhaps more so than other disciplines, must be connected to its history.

Because of misconceptions, students (and their parents) often view mathematics as a series of rote procedures and algorithms to be committed to memory. Students consider mathematicians to be exceptional individuals who solve and invent mathematics through sheer thought, with no hint of trial and error or inductive reasoning. The human element in mathematics and the resulting development of mathematical ideas, concepts, and applications are often overlooked. The centuries-old procedures and algorithms of mathematics were in fact developed by individuals of flesh and blood, who had the same human foibles and aspirations as anyone today. Their discoveries were the result of explorations, experimentations, and persistence, in addition to brain power.

Famous Problems and Their Mathematicians will help remedy these misconceptions of mathematics. Each chapter demonstrates an application or exploration of mathematics that is interesting in and of itself, or is connected to a real mathematician whose story should be told. The range and variety of personalities is fascinating. Mathematicians of the past were emperors, housewives, merchants, generals, and future presidents of the United States. Many overcame overwhelming obstacles to succeed at their mathematics, while others were born with a natural talent in the field. Some became involved in mathematics through a series of happy coincidences, while others were clearly born to pursue the discipline.

The wide range of individuals who appear in *Famous Problems and Their Mathematicians* clearly portrays the multicultural origins of mathematics. Several chapters are devoted to Hindu and Islamic mathematicians, such as Bhaskara, Al-Khwarizimi, and Omar Al-Khayyam. The mathematics of Egypt, China, and Armenia appear in other chapters. The women of mathematics, such as Sonya Kovalevsky, Sophie St. Germain, Hypatia, Mary Boole, and Florence Nightingale, are discussed as well. The result is that students will see mathematics as a discipline that transcends culture, time, and gender, and as a discipline for everyone, everywhere.

All students will benefit from learning something about the mathematicians and histories that generated famous mathematics problems. The applications of mathematics presented here demonstrate that the discipline is not devised in a sterile atmosphere with chalk and a blackboard. Rather, the developments in mathematics are nurtured by history and culture. The famous problems show mathematics to be a living discipline, reactive to society and its needs.

Famous Problems and Their Mathematicians contains 61 chapters, each with a problem activity that is generally within the reach of middle school students. Many of the problems are nonroutine and will be challenging even to high school students. The problems are innovative and yet engaging because they do not require rote, algorithmic mathematics. Thus, this book presents a broad range of problems to challenge students in grades 5 through 12.

Each chapter presents the historical background of a mathematician or a problem. The chapters are designed to stand alone, and need not be used in any particular sequence. Each chapter also contains a section for the teacher, including the solution to the student activity and additional historical information. Chapter extensions present related information and an additional problem for students to solve.

Most teachers have a full syllabus. With this is mind, the problems in this book have been designed for easy incorporation into an already crowded curriculum. Each chapter may be used as an introduction to a new topic, as an enrichment project, or as recreational mathematics with something to be learned in the bargain. The problems are arranged in order of the level of mathematics required to solve them. The first few problems may be solved by elementary school students, while the last few are most appropriate for high school students. A point to be made, however, is that students at the elementary level are able to reach beyond those topics that are typically suggested for them. *Famous Problems and Their Mathematicians* provides students the opportunity for such development. Along the same line of thinking, high school students can benefit from problems that may not require upper-level mathematics, but that require them to expand their mathematics applications and think intuitively about a problem situation.

The problems may be assigned to either individual students or small groups of students during a class period, as take-home assignments, or as projects. The projects that may be generated by *Famous Problems and Their Mathematicians* are many. Student presentations, posters, and murals are just a few of the possibilities for teachers. The problem topics range from the whimsical logic problems of Lewis Carroll and the brain teasers of Sam Lloyd, to the mathematics of networks by Leonard Euler and the development of three-dimensional angular deficiency by René Descartes. Chapter extensions might be offered as follow-up activities for the classroom problems.

The student activities in *Famous Problems and Their Mathematicians* meet various national standards of mathematics. In the *1990 Yearbook*, the National Council of Teachers of Mathematics stated, "An awareness of critical events in the history of mathematics, and of the troubled genesis of some specific topics and results, could well complement previous experiences by showing how even great mathematicians had to struggle and use considerable ingenuity to produce what is now accepted as the body of mathematical knowledge." When students can glimpse into the minds of the great mathematicians, they are able to see the human aspect of mathematics through the only too human aspects of its leading practitioners. *Famous Problems and Their Mathematicians* allows students to be great mathematicians as they replicate the discovery processes of René Descartes and Pierre de Fermat, and as they apply mathematics to the real world. When students discover mathematics, they prize it and they remember it. Most important, they appreciate mathematics as a living, growing discipline with applications and relevance to the real world.

Bibliography

Bell, T. E. *Men in Mathematics.* New York: Simon & Schuster, 1937.

Berggren, J. *Episodes in the Mathematics of Medieval Islam.* New York: Springer-Verlag, 1986.

Boyer, Carl. *The History of Mathematics.* New York: John Wiley, 1968.

Burton, David M. *The History of Mathematics: An Introduction.* Boston: Allyn & Bacon, 1978.

Cajori, Florian. *A History of Mathematics Notation.* New York: Dover, 1993.

Dunham, William. *Journey Through Genius—The Great Theorems of Mathematics.* New York: John Wiley, 1990.

Eves, Howard W. *In Mathematical Circles.* Boston: Prindle, Weber & Smith, 1969.

———. *Mathematical Circles Revisited.* Boston: Prindle, Weber & Smith, 1971.

Gjertsen, Derek. *The Newton Handbook.* London: Routledge & Kegan Paul, 1986.

Heath, Thomas L. *A History of Greek Mathematics, Volumes I and II.* New York: Dover, 1981.

Johnson, Art. *Classic Math: History Topics for the Classroom.* Palo Alto, CA: Dale Seymour, 1994.

Loomis, Elisha Scott. *The Pythagorean Proposition.* Reston, VA: National Council of Teachers of Mathematics, 1968.

National Council of Teachers of Mathematics. *Historical Topics for the Mathematics Classroom.* Reston, VA: National Council of Teachers of Mathematics, 1973.

Olivastro, Dominic. *Ancient Puzzles: Classic Brainteasers and Other Timeless Mathematical Games of the Last 10 Centuries.* New York: Bantam Books, 1994.

Osen, Lynn M. *Women in Mathematics.* Cambridge, MA: MIT Press, 1974.

Pappas, Theoni. *The Joy of Mathematics.* San Carlos, CA: Wide World, 1986.

———. *More Joy of Mathematics.* San Carlos, CA: Wide World, 1991.

Perl, Teri H., and Joan M. Manning. *Women, Numbers and Dreams: Biographical Sketches and Math Activities.* Santa Rosa, CA: National Women's History Project, 1982.

Reimer, Wilbert, and Luetta Reimer. *Historical Connections in Mathematics: Resources for Using History of Mathematics in the Classroom.* Fresno, CA: AIMS Educational Foundation, 1994.

Smith, Sanderson. *Agnesi to Zero: Over 100 Vignettes from the History of Math.* Berkeley, CA: Key Curriculum Press, 1996.

Swetz, Frank J. *Learning Activities from the History of Mathematics.* Portland, ME: J. Weston Walsh, 1994.

———, ed. *From Five Fingers to Infinity: A Journey Through the History of Mathematics.* Chicago: Open Court, 1994.

Time Line

Date	Name	Origin	Page
c.1650 B.C.	A'hmose	Egyptian	100
c.624–547 B.C.	Thales of Miletus	Greek	84
c.570–500 B.C.	Pythagoras	Greek	155
c.429–348 B.C.	Plato	Greek	138
287–212 B.C.	Archimedes	Greek	89
c.276–195 B.C.	Eratosthenes	Greek	38, 87
c.60–c.120	Nicomachus of Gerasa	Syrian	51, 59
c.65–c.125	Heron of Alexandria	Greek	126
c.70–c.135	Theon of Smyrna	Greek	51
c.200–c.284	Diophantus	Greek	132
c.290–c.350	Pappus	Greek	158
370–415	Hypatia of Alexandria	Greek	41
476–550	Aryabhata	Indian	106
598–670	Brahmagupta	Hindu	108
735–804	Alcuin of York	European	116
c.790–c.840	Al-Khwarizimi	Persian	119
940–998	Abu'l-Wafa'	Islamic	164
1044–1130	Omar Al-Khayyam	Persian	163
1114–1185	Bhaskara Acharya	Hindu	142
c.1175–1228	Leonardo of Pisa	Italian	44
1290–1349	Thomas Bradwardine	English	13
1436–1476	Johann Müller (Regiomontanus)	German	144
1448–1500	Nicholas Chuquet	French	55
1452–1519	Leonardo da Vinci	Italian	146, 157
1480–1520	Estienne de La Roche	French	55
1486–1567	Michael Stifel	German	122
c.1500–1557	Nicolo Fortuna (Tartaglia)	Italian	52
1501–1576	Girolamo Cardano	Italian	5, 53
1510–1558	Robert Recorde	English	112
1537–1612	Christopher Clavius	German	9
1540–1603	François Vieta	French	3
1540–1610	Ludoph van Ceulen	German	27
1564–1642	Galileo Galilei	Italian	90, 96
1588–1648	Marin Mersenne	French	49
1596–1650	René Descartes	French	69, 102
1598–1647	Bonaventura Cavalieri	Italian	95
1601–1665	Pierre de Fermat	French	82, 170
1602–1675	Gilles Personne de Roberval	French	95
1605–1675	Bernard Frenicle de Bessey	French	172
1622–1703	Vincenzo Viviani	Italian	149
1623–1662	Blaise Pascal	French	62, 153
1642–1727	Sir Isaac Newton	English	129
1654–1722	Pierre Varignon	French	151

Date	Name	Origin	Page
1667–1748	Johann Bernoulli	Swiss	166
1687–1768	Roger Simson	English	165
1690–1764	Christian Goldbach	Russian	81
1706–1790	Benjamin Franklin	American	92
1707–1783	Leonhard Euler	Swiss	72, 81, 168
1707–1788	George Louis Leclerc, Compte de Buffon	French	24
1718–1799	Maria Gaetana Agnesi	Italian	134
1731–1806	Benjamin Bannekar	American	114
1743–1794	Marie Jean Antoine Nicolas de Caritat Condorcet	French	28
1746–1818	Gaspard Monge	French	152
1749–1827	Pierre La Place	French	26
1750–1800	Lorenzo Mascheroni	Italian	161
1768–1830	Joseph Fourier	French	15
1768–1843	William E. Wallace	English	165
1769–1821	Napoleon Bonaparte	French	161
1771–1859	Joseph-Dias Gergonne	French	159
1776–1831	Sophie St. Germain	French	17
1777–1855	Carl Friedrich Gauss	German	11, 18, 66
1777–1859	Louis Poinsot	French	13
1785–1864	Charles Julien Branchion	French	152
1788–1867	Jean Victor Poncelet	French	173
1789–1857	Augustin Cauchy	French	15
1790–1868	August Möbius	German	1
1792–1856	Nicolai Lobachevsky	Russian	78
1798–1880	Michael Chasles	French	124
1800–1834	Karl Wilhelm Feurbach	German	174
1802–1860	Janos Bolyai	Hungarian	78
1805–1865	William Rowan Hamilton	Irish	74
1806–1871	Augustus De Morgan	British	32
1811–1832	Evariste Galois	French	15
1812–1882	William Shanks	British	27
1814–1877	J. J. Sylvester	British	30
1815–1864	George Boole	British	6
1820–1910	Florence Nightingale	British	30
1826–1866	G. F. B. Riemann	German	80
1831–1881	James A. Garfield	American	162
1832–1898	Charles Dodgson	English	20
1832–1916	Mary Everest Boole	British	6
1834–1923	John Venn	English	35
1841–1911	Sam Loyd	American	97
1850–1891	Sonya Kovalevsky	Russian	42
1857–1930	Henry Ernest Dudeney	British	99
1859–1943	Georg Alexander Pick	Austrian	57
1862–1943	David Hilbert	German	158
1877–1947	G. H. Hardy	British	47
1885–1977	John Littlewood	British	47
1887–1920	Srinivasa Ayanger Ramanujan	Indian	47

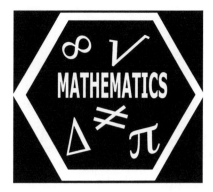

Mathematics by Accident

Do you know what flypaper is? It is a long strip of paper with a sticky surface for catching flies. It is hung from a ceiling but is difficult to handle because it is so sticky. Flypaper helped create a new field of mathematics. Sometimes, as for the German mathematician and astronomer August Möbius (1790–1868), discoveries in mathematics happen by accident.

In 1858 Möbius, retired from astronomy and mathematics, was on vacation with his wife when he made the discovery that made him famous. Möbius and his wife had rented a small cabin in the woods. The cabin had no screens, so flying insects were a problem. The two vacationers decided to hang flypaper from the ceiling to catch the insects, but Möbius was so tall that he kept bumping into the flypaper. He tried to shorten the flypaper strips by forming them into loops, but this didn't work because the flypaper stuck to itself. Finally, Möbius arrived at a solution: Twist one end of the strip before forming the loop (see the figure below). The twist kept the flypaper from sticking to itself.

One evening, Möbius was staring at one of his twisted flypaper loops and realized that it possessed some amazing properties. Discover some of them for yourself. Make a Möbius Band by cutting a strip of paper about 12 inches long and 1 inch wide. Hold one end of the strip while twisting the other end 180°, and then attach the ends together. It should look like this:

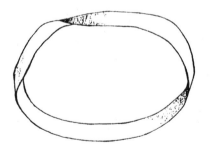

Try the following tasks with your Möbius Band. Can you predict the result of each task?

1. Draw a line along the middle of the band. Continue drawing until you meet the beginning of your line. What do you notice?

2. Cut the Möbius Band along the line you drew. What happens?

3. Make another Möbius Band and draw a line along it, at a distance from the edge of 1/3 the width of the band. Continue drawing until you meet the beginning of your line. Cut along this line. What is the result?

Mathematics by Accident
Teacher Page

Students will discover that a line drawn along the middle of a Möbius Band forms a closed loop. This proves that a Möbius Band has a single surface, not two surfaces as for the more familiar type of band known as a ring. This is what first intrigued Möbius about his flypaper loops. When students cut along the middle of the Möbius Band, the result is a single but longer Möbius Band. Cutting along a line drawn at a distance from the edge of 1/3 the width of the band produces a larger Möbius Band, interlocked with a smaller Möbius Band with a double twist.

The flypaper Möbius Band was the beginning of a new field of mathematics—topology. At 68, an age when most people have retired from their professions, Möbius began writing about topology. He devoted the last 10 years of his life to the study of topology, and became well known for his discoveries in this field.

Although the Möbius Band is interesting in and of itself, it has beneficial, real-world applications. A drive belt or pulley in the form of a Möbius Band will outlast a traditional drive belt or pulley. Because a Möbius belt or pulley has a single surface, the wear occurs evenly. For a traditional belt or pulley, the wear occurs only on the inside surface.

Extension

There is an interesting pattern for "descendant" bands of the Möbius Band. When a two-surfaced ring is cut along the middle, the result is two separate rings. When a Möbius Band is cut along the middle, the result is a larger Möbius Band. Have students continue to explore this result with further generations of the Möbius Band. What happens when a Möbius Band with two half-twists (each half-twist is 180°) is cut along the middle? What happens to a band with three half-twists? Four half-twists? Have students look for a pattern in their results, and then generalize the pattern to determine the result for a Super Möbius Band descendant, one with 45 half-twists.

Students will discover that when the number of half-twists in the original Möbius Band is odd, cutting results in a single band, with the number of twists in the resulting band related to the number of half-twists in the original Möbius Band. One half-twist in the original Möbius Band produces four half-twists in the resulting band. Three half-twists in the original band produce eight half-twists in the resulting band. Five half-twists in the original produce 12 half-twists in the resulting band. This pattern continues so that an original band with 45 half-twists produces a band with 92 half-twists. When the number of half-twists in the original Möbius Band is even, cutting results in two interlocked bands, with the same number of half-twists in each resulting band as in the original Möbius Band.

Leave No Problem Unsolved

The sixteenth century was a time of tension between two great superpowers. Spain and France were technically at peace, but war was a constant threat. Any information about the enemy was invaluable, especially intercepted messages. The Spanish wrote all their messages in codes that seemed impossible to break. Their keys, or ciphers, to the codes were 100 characters in length, but the Spanish were not prepared for François Vieta (1540–1603). He managed to break each and every code the Spanish tried, no matter how complex. Vieta was so successful that Spanish King Philip II complained to the pope that the French were using magic and sorcery, "contrary to the Christian Faith."

It wasn't sorcery, but mathematics. Vieta was a capable mathematician who wrote about geometry, trigonometry, and arithmetic. In one of his books, he wrote that his life's goal was to leave no problem unsolved. In *Artem Analyticam Isagoge* (1591), Vieta was the first mathematician to use letters as variables to represent quantities. His system for variables used vowels for unknown values, and consonants for known values. This breakthrough in mathematics notation made possible rapid advancements in mathematics. Vieta's breakthrough also began a flood of mathematical symbols. Nearly all the mathematical symbols used today were invented within 100 years of the publication of his book.

In 1594 Vieta demonstrated his outstanding mathematical ability in a contest with Dutch mathematician Adriaen Van Rooman. This wasn't just a contest between two mathematicians. It was a contest between the best mathematicians in two countries, France and Holland. Van Rooman presented Vieta with a problem and one of its solutions. Van Rooman placed two other solutions he had found in a sealed envelope and challenged Vieta to find these solutions. The problem Van Rooman presented to Vieta was the following equation:

$$45x - 3,795x^3 + 95,634x^5 - 1,138,500x^7 + 7,811,375x^9 - 34,512,075x^{11} +$$
$$105,306,075x^{13} - 2,826,762,810x^{15} + 384,942,375x^{17} - 4,884,494,125x^{19}$$
$$+ 483,841,800x^{21} - 378,658,800x^{23} + 236,030,652x^{25} - 117,679,100x^{27} +$$
$$46,955,700x^{29} - 14,945,040x^{31} + 3,764,565x^{33} - 740,259x^{35} + 111,150x^{37}$$
$$- 12,300x^{39} + 945x^{41} - 45x^{43} + x^{45} = a$$

Leave No Problem Unsolved continues on page 4.

Van Rooman provided Vieta with the solution when $a = \sqrt{1\frac{3}{4} - \sqrt{\frac{5}{16}} - \sqrt{1\frac{7}{8} - \sqrt{\frac{45}{64}}}}$

At first, Vieta was unable to find any solutions involving sines of multiple arcs, but then he saw an underlying mathematical relationship and found not only Van Rooman's two solutions but also 22 others! He won the contest for France.

Secret messages sent by modern governments involve numerical relationships that even high-speed computers can't break. Less secret messages don't need to be so complex. One simple way to write a coded message is to replace each letter in the original message with a different letter according to a cipher. For example, I LOVE MATH becomes K NQXG OCVJ with a cipher that replaces each letter in the original message with the letter that occurs two places later in the alphabet. For example, the letter *I* is replaced with *K*, the letter that occurs two places later in the alphabet. For this activity, write a brief message and devise a cipher to encode it. Give the coded message and the cipher to a classmate.

From *Famous Problems and Their Mathematicians*. © 1999 Art Johnson. Teacher Ideas Press. (800) 237-6124.

Leave No Problem Unsolved
Teacher Page

Vieta was not only a mathematician but a trained lawyer. He spent nearly 10 years as a lawyer after graduating from the University of Poitiers with a degree in law. Vieta also wrote a number of books about astronomy. It was his ability to decipher codes, however, that earned him the respect and gratitude of the French government.

Another mathematician who worked with codes was Girolamo Cardano (1501–1576), one of the most interesting characters in the history of mathematics. He was a professor of mathematics at the Universities of Milan, Bologna, and then Padua. At each university, he left under the shadow of one scandal or another. Cardano wrote about mathematics, medicine, alchemy, astrology, and astronomy. He was as famous for his medicine as for his mathematics. He traveled to Scotland to treat the archbishop of Edinburgh (successfully), and was invited to be court physician for the king of Denmark and also papal physician for the pope. Cardano wrote the first psychology book, *Comfort*, which became a best-seller. In a seventeenth-century illustration Hamlet is pictured holding a copy of *Comfort* during his famous soliloquy.

Cardano's great mathematics work was *Ars Magna* (1545), in which he demonstrated how to solve cubic and quartic equations using radicals. Cardano's solutions were not original, but his clarity made *Ars Magna* a milestone in the history of mathematics. Soon after its publication, Cardano became a professor of medicine at the University of Padua.

Controversies began to plague Cardano. Nicolo Tartaglia accused him of plagiarism in *Ars Magna* (see "A Difficult Childhood," p. 52). It wasn't entirely true. Although Cardano broke a promise not to reveal Tartaglia's method of solving cubic equations, Cardano did duly credit him in several footnotes. In 1560, Cardano's son was executed for attempting to poison his wife. In 1570, Cardano was imprisoned by the Inquisition for heresy. It seems Cardano had cast Jesus Christ's horoscope. Amid all these scandals were numerous affairs and bouts of drinking.

Cardano's method of sending a coded message was to design a grille that, when superimposed on a seemingly innocent message, revealed the letters that spelled out the secret message, as shown below. Explain Cardano's Grille to your students and have them design a secret message, contained within an innocent message, and the grille that reveals the secret message.

This has been the nicest vacation I have had in a long time.

The hotel is really grand and is perfect.

Aunt May

Mary Boole's Cards

Mary Everest Boole (1832–1916) was only 32 when her life changed forever. She was the mother of five children and happily married when her husband, mathematician George Boole (1815–1864), suddenly died. In England of the 1860s, the prospects for a widow with five young children were not promising. There were few jobs available to women, and those that were didn't pay well.

Instead of idly worrying about her future, Mary found a job as a librarian at Queen's College in London. Soon after, she began work as a schoolteacher. While she was a teacher, Mary invented her Boole Cards (an example is shown below). She thought that Boole Cards were the perfect way for women of her time to develop their knowledge and talents at home, "without agitation or public discussion . . . or acts of Parliament." In other words, her cards would provide interesting amusement for women and their children, without requiring women to leave their homes or neglect their families. The women could produce beautiful designs while learning something about mathematics, without any disruption of English society.

Mary designed her Boole Cards so that yarn or thread could be used to connect points with matching numbers. For this activity, use a pencil or pen to connect each pair of matching points along the "arms" of the figure below. When you have finished, you might shade alternating areas of the design to improve its appearance.

Now, design a Boole Card of your own. Experiment by varying the angle between the arms or changing the spacing between the points. Try using different spacing along each arm, or random spacing.

You may have noticed that Mary Boole's middle name, Everest, is also the name of a mountain in Asia—the highest mountain in the world. Mary's maiden name was Everest. Mount Everest was named after her uncle, George Everest, who led a surveying expedition to that peak.

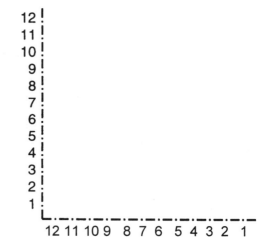

Mary Boole's Cards
Teacher Page

The student activity will result in the following design:

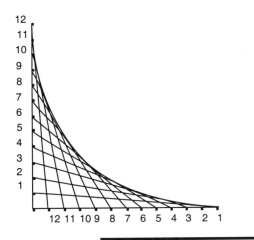

George Boole's death was not only sudden, it was unnecessary. Boole died of pneumonia that developed from a chill. It seems Boole took a long walk before his scheduled lecture at the University of Cork in Ireland. He was caught in a downpour. Rather than return home, change clothes, and be late for his lecture, he walked two miles to the classroom and delivered his lecture soaking wet. He developed a chill that became a fever, and the fever, in turn, developed into pneumonia. Mary Boole's cure for her husband's chill was to fight fire with fire: She would cure it the same way he caught it. She kept her husband in a bed with wet sheets to simulate his wet clothes. He never recovered. George Boole was a moderately well known mathematician when he died. It was not until a century later that his algebra, called Boolean Algebra, found a real-world application: The logic of Boolean Algebra is the logic of computer programming.

George Boole, a self-made man, was born to a poor shoemaker. He studied at the National Primary School but received little formal education after graduating. Boole realized that education was the key to success, though, and taught himself mathematics because he could not afford to attend a university. By the age of 25, he was discovering original mathematics. In 1844, the Royal Society gave him a gold medal for a paper about the calculus of operations.

In 1854, Boole published *An Investigation of the Laws of Thought, on Which Are Founded the Mathematical Theories of Logic and Probabilities*, certainly the longest-titled important mathematics work. In *Laws of Thought*, Boole fully explained his symbolic algebra. He clearly demonstrated that the logical reasoning of Aristotle could be represented in algebraic equations. According to Boole, "We ought no longer to associate Logic and Metaphysics, but Logic and Mathematics."

Mary Boole's Cards Teacher Page continues on page 8.

Extension

Boolean Algebra is based on the operations AND and OR between two sets. For example, if $A = \{1,2,3\}$ and $B = \{3,4,5\}$, then:

$$A \text{ AND } B = \{3\} \qquad A \text{ OR } B = \{1,2,3,4,5\}$$

The set A AND B contains all the members that belong to both set A and set B. The set A OR B contains all the members that belong to either set A or set B.

Explain the basis of Boolean Algebra to your students and ask them to find the AND and OR sets for each of the following pairs of sets:

1. $A = \{a,b,c,d,e\}$ $B = \{c,d,e,f,g\}$
2. $A = \{1,3,5,7,9\}$ $B = \{2,4,6,8,9\}$
3. $A = \{2,4,6,8, ...\}$ $B = \{1,3,5,7, ...\}$
4. $A = \{1,4,9,16\}$ $B = \{1,3,5,7,9,11,13,15\}$

Solutions

1. A AND $B = \{c,d,e\}$ A OR $B = \{a,b,c,d,e,f,g\}$
2. A AND $B = \{9\}$ A OR $B = \{1,2,3,4,5,6,7,8,9\}$
3. A AND $B = \{\varnothing\}$ A OR $B = \{1,2,3,4, ...\}$

$\varnothing$ represents the empty set and is used to indicate that a problem has no solution.

4. A AND $B = \{1,9\}$ A OR $B = \{1,3,4,5,7,9,11,13,15,16\}$

A Very Important Date

Have you noticed that the day of the week of every calendar date changes every year? For example, if your birthday is on a Wednesday this year, it will fall on a different day of the week next year. If our calendar year were 365 days every year, it would be fairly easy to determine on what day a particular calendar date would fall, such as for your 21st birthday. However, because every fourth year is a leap year (an extra day is inserted into the calendar as February 29), determining the day of the week for a specific calendar date is much more complex.

Many mathematicians have solved problems involving calendar dates. In fact, our present calendar, called the Gregorian calendar (named after Pope Gregory XIII), was designed by Jesuit mathematician and astronomer Christopher Clavius (1537–1612) in 1572. Clavius included a leap year so that the calendar would be more accurate. Even with the extra day of a leap year, Clavius's calendar still needed frequent adjustment. To make his calendar even more accurate, Clavius added another stipulation: A century year, such as 1600 or 1700, would be a leap year only if it were divisible by 400. For example, 1600 was a leap year, but 1700 was not.

Because of the leap year rule, determining the day of the week for a specific calendar date is more complex. For this activity, determine the day of the week for each of the following events:

1. 4 July 1776—The first Independence Day.

2. 14 April 1912—The day the *Titanic* struck an iceberg.

3. 10 July 1969—The day Neil Armstrong walked on the moon.

4. 19 November 1863—The day Lincoln delivered the "Gettysburg Address."

5. Your birthday.

6. The day of your 21st birthday.

7. Any important historical date.

Use the following formula to determine the days of the week for the above events.

$$t = d + 2m + \frac{3m + 3}{5} + y + \frac{y}{4} - \frac{y}{100} + \frac{y}{400} + 2$$

A Very Important Date continues on page 10.

The variables represent the following:

t = total

d = calendar date of the month (for example, March 15 has a value of 15)

m = month of the year, beginning with a value of 3 for March (April has a value of 4, May has a value of 5, and so forth; using this method, January has a value of 13, not 1; and February has a value of 14, not 2)

y = year of the calendar date, except for a January or February date, in which case the previous year is the value (for example, the date January 15, 1995, has a value of 1,994)

To evaluate t, find the sum of all the terms. If a term is not an integer, round down to the nearest integer (for example, if

$$\frac{y}{4} = 500.75$$

use a value of 500 for that term). The last step is to divide t by 7 and record the remainder as an integer. The remainder determines the day of the week for the event: 0 = Saturday, 1 = Sunday, 2 = Monday, 3 = Tuesday, 4 = Wednesday, 5 = Thursday, 6 = Friday.

A Very Important Date
Teacher Page

The days of the week for the student activity are as follows:

1. 4 July 1776—Thursday
2. 14 April 1912—Sunday
3. 10 July 1969—Thursday
4. 19 November 1863—Thursday

Students might wonder why our calendar is named after Pope Gregory. Actually, he wasn't the first pope involved with the mathematics of the calendar. As early as 1545, the Council of Trent decreed that the calendar then in use, the Julian calendar, needed revision. Pope Paul III had noticed that on the first day of spring (March 21) in 1545, sunlight did not shine through the window of a church as expected. In fact, it was not until 10 days later that the sunlight fell upon the window as expected. This meant that the calendar was premature by 10 days. With an inaccurate calendar, it would be impossible to properly observe church holy days. This prompted Paul to convene a meeting of the Council of Trent, where the decision was made to revise the existing calendar.

It was not until nearly 30 years later that the revisions actually took effect. By then, Gregory was pope, and he commissioned Clavius to revise the calendar. Clavius, aided by fellow clerics, constructed a calendar that was more accurate than the existing Julian calendar. Whereas the Julian calendar lost 11 minutes, 45 seconds each year, resulting in a loss of 10 days in 16 centuries, the new calendar lost less than 30 seconds per year, and would not need any adjustments for 3,323 years. In 1582, Gregory finally issued a papal bull (decree) declaring the Julian calendar null and void and establishing the new Gregorian calendar in its place. The immediate effect was that the day following October 5, 1582, was October 15, 1582. Thus, the lost 10 days were restored, but not in all countries. It was not until 1752 that England changed to the Gregorian calendar. The change came even later for other countries: China in 1912, and Greece in 1923.

Extension

The date for Easter, an important holy day for Christians, is difficult to determine. In brief, it falls on the first Sunday following the first full moon that occurs on or after the first day of spring (March 21). Carl Friedrich Gauss (1777–1855) found an algorithm for determining the date of Easter. Have students use Gauss's algorithm to determine the date of the next Easter, or for any year in the past or future. Many commercial calendars show the dates of Easter for future years, and so may be used to verify students' calculations.

A Very Important Date Teacher Page continues on page 12.

---

1. Determine integers for the variables m and n using the following table:

Years	m	n
1582–1699	22	2
1700–1799	23	3
1800–1899	24	4
1900–2000	24	5
2001–2100	25	6

2. Find a, the integer remainder after dividing the year by 4.

3. Find b, the integer remainder after dividing the year by 7.

4. Find c, the integer remainder after dividing the year by 19.

5. Find d, the integer remainder after dividing $(19c + m)$ by 30.

6. Find e, the integer remainder after dividing $(2a + 4b + 6d + n)$ by 7.

7. Easter falls in either March $(22 + d + e)$ or April $(d + e - 9)$. If $(22 + d + e)$ is less than 32, then $(22 + d + e)$ is the March date for Easter. If $(22 + d + e)$ is ≤ 32, then $(d + e - 9)$ is the April date for Easter.

A Rediscovery Leads to Fame

Sometimes discoveries were made in mathematics only to be lost or forgotten, and then rediscovered by someone else. That's just what happened with star polygons.

Star polygons were discovered by Thomas Bradwardine (1290–1349), an English theologian who served the church in many positions, including confessor to King Edward III. In 1349, he reached the peak of success. He was appointed archbishop of Canterbury, the highest church office in England. His joy was short-lived: Bradwardine died of the Black Death one month after taking office. When he died, his mathematics writings were lost in the books and scrolls of the church, not to be seen again for centuries.

Nearly 500 years later, French mathematician Louis Poinsot (1777–1859) rediscovered Bradwardine's polygons and gave them the name they have today—star polygons. It was some years after Poinsot's death that Bradwardine's writings about star polygons were discovered.

One of Poinsot's star polygons is shown below. To form this star polygon, the circle was divided into eight congruent arcs, creating eight points spaced equally apart around the circumference of the circle. Then, every third point was connected. Accordingly, this polygon is known as an (8,3) star polygon.

For this activity, design your own star polygon. Divide a circle into an odd number, n, of congruent arcs. Choose an even number, m, so that m and n are relatively prime. Two numbers are relatively prime if their greatest common divisor is 1, such as 8 and 15.

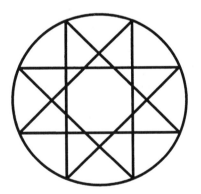

Include the mathematics notation for the polygon: (n,m). Try shading or coloring the various regions of your star polygon to enhance your design.

A Rediscovery Leads to Fame
Teacher Page

Certainly, your students will design a variety of star polygons. One well-known star polygon is the (5,2) star polygon, the traditional five-pointed star:

Bradwardine was so respected for his learning that he became known as Doctor Profundus. His writings, typically concerned with the mathematics of trade and church matters, reflected the times in which he lived. He was the first English mathematician to write about the trigonometry of the Arabic mathematicians.

Poinsot wrote about celestial mechanics and number theory, but he is best known for his discoveries in geometry. He discovered three-dimensional counterparts to his star polygons—polyhedrons. In the case of concave polyhedrons, Poinsot discovered the last two regular polyhedrons: the great dodecahedron and the great icosahedron.

Extension

In the activity, students were directed to choose an odd number for n and an even number for m. These directions ensure that n and m will be prime to each other, or relatively prime (two numbers are relatively prime if their greatest common divisor is 1). If n and m are not relatively prime, the result can be at least two distinct overlapping polygons, as for an (8,2) star polygon:

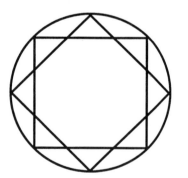

Values for m and n that result in more than one polygon can be as visually pleasing as those values that produce star polygons.

Have students draw an (8,2) star polygon and a (9,3) star polygon and then compare their results with the star polygons they drew for the activity. Ask them to make a conjecture about their results and the values for n and m. If n and m are relatively prime, the result is a single star polygon. If m is a factor of n, then the result is at least two star polygons.

A Promising Career Cut Short

It was his last night on earth. He was sure of that. If his life were to mean anything, he had to write down all the mathematics he had discovered. Someone would learn of his achievements, but did he have enough time?

Did French mathematician Evariste Galois (1811–1832) really spend the last few hours of his life doing mathematics? What would you do if you had only a few hours to live? Probably not mathematics. Besides, how could Galois have been so sure that that night would be his last?

The story begins 10 years earlier. Young Galois was a brilliant student in school, better in mathematics than any of his teachers. When he graduated, Galois applied to the École Polytechnique. A professor interviewed him but could not understand Galois's verbal and chalkboard explanations of his new mathematics—abstract algebra. One thing led to another until Galois lost his temper. The interview ended when Galois threw the eraser and chalk at the poor professor. Galois wasn't accepted to the École Polytechnique.

By the time Galois was 17, he had developed and refined enough of his new mathematics to write a paper about it. He sent this paper to Augustin Cauchy (1789–1857), a member of the Academy of Science. Cauchy lost the paper, and then misplaced a second copy Galois sent him a few weeks later. Some months afterward, Galois wrote an improved paper, this time submitting it to Joseph Fourier (1768–1830), the secretary of the Academy. Fourier died before he could read it, and the paper was never found. One year later, Galois submitted still another paper to the Academy. This time, finally, someone read it. Unfortunately, the reader couldn't understand it and refused to publish the paper.

By now, Galois was upset with the Academy, the government, and anyone else who crossed his path. He vented his frustration on everyone around him. For a group of soldiers stationed in his town, Galois eventually became too much to bear. They plotted to get rid of him, and succeeded in arranging a duel at dawn between Galois and their best marksman, Perscheux d'Herbinville. Galois knew he had no chance of winning, and so, the night before the duel, he hurried to finish his final notebook. Galois was right about the duel: He was shot, and he died the next day. Eventually, his papers, including what he wrote that last night, were published for all to read and admire. Today, a statue of Galois stands in his home town as a tribute to his abstract algebra. Imagine the mathematics he would have discovered had his life not been cut short at only 20 years.

A Promising Career Cut Short continues on page 16.

The mathematics of abstract algebra involves complex concepts called groups. For example, the corners of the Pentagon in Washington, D.C., might be numbered as follows:

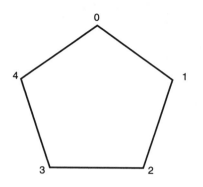

These five vertex points constitute a group. If you were to begin at vertex #2 and travel four vertex points in a clockwise direction, you would arrive at vertex #1. In other words, 2 + 4 = 1 in this group! The table below shows the various results of addition in this group. For this activity, complete the table, and then make a table for addition in a different group.

+	0	1	2	3	4
0					
1					
2					1
3					
4			1		

A Promising Career Cut Short
Teacher Page

The table below shows the results for the student activity. A group of this type is also known as a modular group, and arithmetic in such a group is known as modular arithmetic. The tables for the student activity are modulo 5 tables.

+	0	1	2	3	4
0	0	1	2	3	4
1	1	2	3	4	0
2	2	3	4	0	1
3	3	4	0	1	2
4	4	0	1	2	3

The particular events that resulted in the fatal duel will never be known. Nevertheless, the soldiers' plot likely involved a woman, Stephanie Felice du Motel. One theory is that she flirted with Galois, who returned her attentions. Perscheux d'Herbinville claimed du Motel as his fiancée and demanded satisfaction—a duel with pistols.

Another mathematician who studied the mathematics of groups was Sophie St. Germain (1776–1831), one of France's greatest mathematicians. She was born at a time when mathematics was considered too rigorous for young women. Not so for Sophie St. Germain. She enjoyed mathematics and insisted on studying it. Her parents were aghast at such a thing and forbade her to pursue mathematics. To be sure she complied, they sent her to bed in an unheated room, with no lamp, and only her nightshirt for clothing. They thought that she couldn't possibly manage any mathematics there. How wrong they were. The next morning, they found her sitting at her desk, wrapped in a blanket, fast asleep, with a pen in her hand. On the desk were a smuggled candle, a frozen inkwell, and a page full of calculations. Sophie's parents realized she had a unique ability and agreed to allow her to continue her study of mathematics, in a heated room with plenty of lamps.

Extension

Groups may also be formed by different operations on a group's members. The table below shows the multiplication table for the modulo 5 group. Present an incomplete version of this table to your students and ask them to complete it.

x	0	1	2	3	4
0	0	0	0	0	0
1	0	1	2	3	4
2	0	2	4	1	3
3	0	3	1	4	2
4	0	4	3	2	1

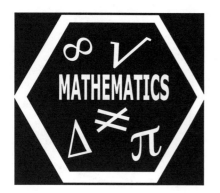

There It Lies

If ever a person was born brilliant, it was German mathematician Carl Friedrich Gauss (1777–1855), known as the Prince of Mathematicians. When Carl was only three years old, he began helping his father with the payroll accounts for his father's modest brickyard business. He even found mistakes that his father had made in the accounts. Later in life, Gauss remembered he could "reckon" before he could even talk. Gauss's genius was not just in mathematics. By the time he was 19, Gauss could speak Spanish, German, Greek, Latin, English, French, and Danish!

When Carl was 10, he again showed his great mathematical ability. On the first day of school, Carl's teacher, Mr. Buttner, gave the class an assignment. Buttner wanted to keep his third-grade students busy while he made a seating chart and recorded the students' names into his rank book. The assignment he gave them was to add all the integers from 1 to 100.

Carl thought about the problem for a few seconds, picked up his slate and chalk, and wrote an answer. He put down the slate and said, "There it lies." Quite some time later, when all the other students in the class had finished, Mr. Buttner asked for answers. Carl's was the only correct answer. Can you think of a way to add all the integers from 1 to 100 without using a calculator?

For this activity, look for number patterns, as young Carl did, to make the problem easier. Check your answer with a calculator. When you have found a method that produces the correct answer, try to find a general rule for adding the first n positive integers (in other words, for adding the integers from 1 to n). Use your rule to add the integers from 1 to 200, or from 1 to 400.

There It Lies
Teacher Page

Gauss probably used the method shown below. He likely paired 1 with 100, 2 with 99, 3 with 98, and so forth: 50 pairs that each total 101. $50 \times 101 = 5{,}050$.

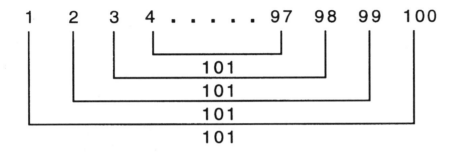

This pattern for the sum of the first n positive integers generalizes into the following formula.

$$\frac{n(n+1)}{2}$$

Gauss was one of the last mathematicians to master all branches of mathematics, and make contributions to all of them. He also made many contributions to science. For example, a measure of electrical energy, the gauss, is named after him. Gauss also speculated about life on other planets. He argued for planting a large forest in the shape of a right triangle with sides in the ratio 3:4:5. Why? So that alien beings living on the moon would see it and realize that intelligent life was present on earth!

Even genius needs a helping hand, however. Gauss's helping hand came from the Duke of Brunswick, a local noble who recognized his genius and supported him financially, allowing Gauss to attend college and devote his time to his study of mathematics. Without the Duke's support, Gauss may have simply been the owner of a successful brickyard.

Extension

Once students have discovered a formula for adding the first n positive integers, have them find a formula for adding the first n positive even integers: $n(n+1)$; and a formula for adding the first n positive odd integers: n^2.

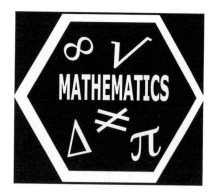

Alice and Mathematics

Thankfully, July 4, 1862, was a beautiful summer's day—a perfect day for a picnic. It's a good thing it was. A rainy day would have ruined everything and changed the history of mathematics and English literature. Charles Dodgson and Roger Duckworth, professors at Trinity College in Cambridge, England, had planned to take the dean's three daughters for a combination boating trip and picnic, and the weather had cooperated. As they boated upriver to their picnic, Dodgson began to amuse the girls with a story, and what a story it was! It featured the adventures of a young girl in a foreign land with all kinds of strange and wondrous creatures. The girls were captivated by the story. Duckworth remembers asking Dodgson if he was making up such a fantastic tale or whether he had heard it when he was a boy. Dodgson assured his friend that he was making up the tale as they rowed. The girls insisted that story continue throughout the picnic, and all the way home.

For days after, the girls talked endlessly about the wonderful story they had heard. Eventually, their father, Henry George Liddel, suggested to Dodgson that he publish his story. Dodgson, a professor of logic, was reluctant to publish a children's story. Liddel insisted, though, and on July 4, 1865, Dodgson presented the dean's oldest daughter, Alice Liddel, with the first copy of the book. He had named the main character after her. *Alice in Wonderland* was an immediate best-seller.

Life was never the same for Charles Dodgson, better known by his pen name, Lewis Carroll (1832–1898). Within two years, Carroll and his character Alice were known across all of Europe. How did the success of *Alice in Wonderland* affect the history of mathematics? Lewis Carroll became so famous that anything he wrote after its publication became popular, including some of his writings about mathematics. What Carroll wrote about mathematics was not the dry logic of his lectures. He composed mind benders, brain teasers, and math puzzles. He made mathematics fun for everyone. Carroll's problems could be solved by the average person, and without a college education. What if it had rained on that July day in 1862? We might not have mathematics brain teasers today, and we certainly wouldn't know Alice, the Cheshire Cat, the Mad Hatter, and the March Hare.

Below are some of Lewis Carroll's brain teasers. For this activity, solve two of them. With each answer, include an explanation of your method for solving the problem.

1. A gentleman had a sitting room with only one window in it—a square window, 3 feet high and 3 feet wide. He had weak eyes, and the window gave too much light. He sent for a builder and told him to alter the window, so as to give half the light. He was to keep the window square, though, and he was to keep it 3 feet high and 3 feet wide. How did he do it? (He wasn't allowed to use curtains, shutters, or colored glass.)

2. Draw three interlaced squares, as shown below, without lifting your pencil from the paper, without retracing any lines, and without crossing any lines.

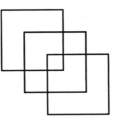

3. Imagine that you have some wooden cubes. You also have six paint tins, each containing a different color of paint. You paint a cube, using a different color on each of its six faces. How many different cubes can you paint, using the same set of six colors?

4. Show that twice the sum of two squares may be written as the sum of two squares.

Alice and Mathematics
Teacher Page

The solutions to the student activity are:

1. The window, still square, is oriented like this:

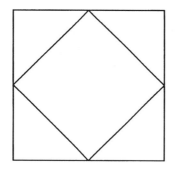

2.

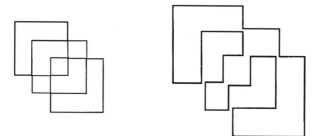

3. 30 differently colored cubes. Assign the six faces a, b, c, d, e, f. For face a opposite face b there are six possible ways to arrange the other four faces. For face a opposite face c there are six possible ways to arrange the other four faces. For face a opposite face d, for face a opposite face e, and for face a opposite face f there are six possible ways to arrange the other four faces. Thus there are 30 differently colored cubes (5×6).

4. Many examples possible: $2(3^2 + 4^2) = 50 = 1 + 49 = 1^2 + 7^2$.

Lewis Carroll's fame allowed him to popularize recreational mathematics in new ways. For example, he published monthly problems in popular magazines, such as *Vanity Fair*. The next issue contained solutions that readers submitted, along with a new problem. He also published the chapters of *A Tangled Tale* in monthly installments, in *The Monthly Packet*. Each chapter ended with a cliffhanger that had to be solved by mathematics; the next chapter contained the solution. Carroll stated that solving these problems served "for the amusement and possible edification of the reader."

Extension

In 1879, Carroll published a new kind of puzzle in *Vanity Fair*, a puzzle he called doublets. He invented the puzzle in response to two young girls who complained that they had nothing to do. The task of the puzzle is to change one word to another word by changing a single letter at a time; each change must form a new word. For example, this is how to change MATH to LOVE:

MATH

MATE

LATE

LANE

LONE

LOVE

Ask students to try to solve the following doublets from Lewis Carroll:
Drive PIG into STY (pig, wig, wag, way, say, sty).
Raise FOUR to FIVE (four, foul, fool, foot, fort, fore, fire, five).
Cover EYE with LID (eye, dye, die, did, lid).
Prove PITY to be GOOD (pity, pits, pins, fins, find, fond, food, good).

Have students make their own doublets for classmates to solve.

π in the Sky

Could that possibly be Buffon, the respected scholar? It can't be—but yes, it definitely is Buffon. Why is he tossing breadsticks over his shoulder onto a tiled floor? Buffon would have explained that he was trying to verify one of his conjectures about the value of π. With breadsticks? Yes, with breadsticks.

George Louis Leclerc, the Compte de Buffon (1707–1788), was a famous scientist and mathematician, known for his discoveries in calculus and natural history. His book *Theorie de la Terre* (1797) greatly influenced a wide range of scientific fields. In his first book, *Sur le Jeu de Franc-Carreau* (1740), Buffon introduced calculus into Probability Theory. In 1777 Buffon proposed randomly tossing a segment onto a series of parallel lines. Buffon believed that the probability of the segment touching any of the parallel lines would involve the value of π. He couldn't prove this conjecture, though, so he conducted an experiment, using breadsticks to represent the segment, and a tiled floor to represent the parallel lines.

Was Buffon's conjecture correct? For this activity, replicate his experiment by following these steps:

1. Break off a 1-inch piece of dry spaghetti.

2. Drop the spaghetti segment onto the series of parallel lines provided on page 25. Record whether the spaghetti segment comes to rest on one of the parallel lines (the try is a "hit") or between the lines (the try is a "miss"). If the spaghetti doesn't come to rest between the two rows of asterisks, the try is invalid and you must drop the spaghetti again.

3. Repeat step 2 until you have a record of 25 valid tries.

4. Use your data to evaluate the following equation:

$$\text{Probability} = 2\left(\frac{\text{hits}}{\text{tries}}\right)$$

_____

_____

_____

_____

_____

_____

π *in the Sky*
Teacher Page

With an infinite number of tosses, the results will show the value of π, a fact that was proven in 1812 by Pierre La Place (1749–1827). The general probability equation is:

$$\text{Probability} = \frac{2l}{\pi d}$$

In this equation, l represents the length of the segment, and d represents the distance between the parallel lines. In the student activity, the experiment is designed so that the result will be the value of π. Combining the data from the entire class will result in an approximation closer to the value of π than will a calculation based on only a single student's data.

Determining ever more accurate representations for π has occupied mathematicians for centuries. Some significant approximations for π include the following:

Archimedes	240 B.C.	$\frac{223}{71}$
Vitruvius	20 B.C.	$3\frac{1}{8}$
Claudius Ptolemy	150	$\frac{377}{120}$
Wang Fan	265	$\frac{142}{45}$
Tsu ch'ung-chih	480	$\frac{355}{113}$
Aryabhata	530	$\frac{62,832}{20,000}$
Brahmagupta	598	$\sqrt{10}$
Bhaskara	1150	$\frac{3,927}{1,250}$
Fibonacci	1200	$\frac{865}{274}$
Dante	1300	$3 + \frac{\sqrt{2}}{10}$

As the approximate value of π became increasingly accurate, mathematicians calculated longer decimal representations. In 1710, Ludoph van Ceulen (1540–1610) computed π to 35 decimal places. In 1873–1874, William Shanks (1812–1882) computed π to 707 decimal places, a record he must have thought would stand for a long time. It lasted until 1945, when John Ferguson, using a desktop calculator, found an error in the 527th place of Shanks's work. With the development of high-speed computers, the accurate computation of π has become less of a mathematical challenge and more of a programming challenge. As of 1999, the world record for the number of digits representing the value of π is 206,158,430,000. Daisuke Takahashi and Yasumasa Kanada used a Hitachi SR3800 at the University of Tokyo to establish their record.

Extension

Have your students find decimal representations of the approximations for π shown above, and then rank the approximations in order of accuracy.

A Mathematician Exposed

How many eggs would you like in your omelet? Be careful: What you answer may cost you your life! This is exactly what happened to French mathematician and social scientist Marie Jean Antoine Nicolas de Caritat Condorcet (1743–1794). Condorcet lost his life because he became involved in politics and liked omelets.

Condorcet studied mathematics and history at several universities. He published a number of books about integral calculus, history, and philosophy. In 1774, he became Inspector General of the mint in France after which he focused his mathematics on social problems.

When the French Revolution erupted in 1789, Condorcet enthusiastically supported the new liberal government. He was elected to the Legislative Assembly and soon after was appointed secretary. Condorcet was one of the representatives who developed plans for a nationwide educational system. Within three years, he was a prominent leader in the government. When the king of France, Louis XVI, was charged with treason, Condorcet was the only member of the Assembly who voted to spare his life. This vote was the beginning of the end for Condorcet.

As the revolution progressed, increasingly radical politics became the rule. During this time, members of the royalty, members of the aristocracy, and even educated citizens were executed as enemies of the state. Condorcet was spared, along with other mathematicians, because mathematics were of service to the new government. Eventually, however, Condorcet was named an enemy of the state and sentenced to death. Condorcet fled Paris and went into hiding. If not for an omelet, he might have escaped his fate.

While traveling in disguise, Condorcet entered an inn and ordered an omelet. The innkeeper asked Condorcet how many eggs he wanted in his omelet, to which Condorcet replied, "A dozen." Condorcet had lived in high society all his life, and he had never prepared his own meals. He had no idea that a dozen eggs would make enough omelets for four or five people. The suspicious innkeeper asked Condorcet his trade. When Condorcet told him he was a carpenter, the innkeeper looked at Condorcet's hands, which were smooth and uncallused. Caught by his reply, Condorcet was arrested and taken to prison. He didn't live to see the next morning. During the night, Condorcet was either poisoned or allowed to commit suicide. In either case, an omelet had cost him his life.

One of Condorcet's most important contributions to mathematics was his method for determining the winner in an election between more than two candidates when none of the candidates win more than half the votes. Condorcet's method for finding the winner was to compare them head-to-head, or pairwise. Any candidate who won every pairwise comparison was the winner.

The following data show the order of voting preference for three candidates in a school election. The first column shows the order of preference for 40 voters. In other words, 40 voters would prefer Candy first, Meagan next, and Bethany last.

40 votes	21 votes	23 votes	18 votes	17 votes	18 votes
Candace	Bethany	Meagan	Meagan	Candace	Bethany
Meagan	Meagan	Candace	Bethany	Bethany	Candace
Bethany	Candace	Bethany	Candace	Meagan	Meagan

To determine the winner, Condorcet would have used a table like the one below to compare each candidate with every other candidate in a pairwise comparison. The table shows the results of the first two sets of votes.

For this activity, use the data and Condorcet's method to complete the table and determine the winner—the candidate who is undefeated in all pairwise comparisons. See figure on page 30.

	Candace vs. Bethany	Candace vs. Meagan	Bethany vs. Meagan
1.	40	40	40
2.	21	21	21
3.			
4.			
5.			
6.			

A Mathematician Exposed
Teacher Page

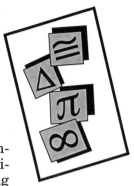

The completed table for the student activity is shown below. Candace receives more votes than Bethany or Meagan in direct competition. In turn, Meagan received more votes than Bethany. By totaling the votes of preference for each pair of girls, the winner can then be determined using Condorcet's method.

	Candace vs. Bethany		Candace vs. Meagan		Bethany vs. Meagan	
1.	40		40			40
2.		21		21	21	
3.	23			23		23
4.		18		18		18
5.	17		17		17	
6.		18	18		18	
Totals	80	57	75	62	56	81

Condorcet was the first mathematician to apply mathematics to social situations. Many others soon followed in this effort. One of the most unexpected persons to use mathematics in social situations was not even a mathematician, but a nurse, Florence Nightingale (1820–1910), who invented a new way to display data—the pie chart.

Nightingale was born to a comfortable, middle-class life and was expected to pursue activities appropriate for young women in Victorian England, but she had other interests. She studied mathematics and natural sciences, and soon decided to pursue a nursing career. In 1849, she traveled across Europe, observing hospital practices. When the Crimean War erupted in 1854, Nightingale traveled to the war front to tend to the wounded and dying.

The loss of life in army hospitals was horrific, but without specific changes in procedures, nothing could be done. Nightingale collected, tabulated, and interpreted statistics, and became convinced that proper sanitation and nursing practices could help. When she initiated sanitation procedures in her own hospital, the mortality rate fell from 45% to 2% in only a few weeks. Nightingale had used mathematics to develop a solution to a social problem, but she still needed a method for displaying her statistics that would convince her superiors that the changes were necessary. Nightingale invented the pie chart as a way to represent her data. It was the pie chart display of her statistics that finally convinced the military authorities, then Parliament, and then Queen Victoria that Nightingale's suggested improvements were desperately needed. Interestingly, Nightingale's childhood mathematics tutor, J. J. Sylvester (1814–1877), coined the word *graph* (*Chemistry in Algebra*, 1877) to represent a pictorial display of data.

After the war, Nightingale founded the Nightingale School and Home for Nurses in London, the first such school ever established. For a career of dedicated service to others, Nightingale was awarded the British Order of Merit. She was the first woman to receive the award.

Extension

Have your students survey students in other classes about their favorite flavor of ice cream, M&M color, music band, television show, or some other topic, and then display the data in a pie chart. Students may make the pie chart using graphing software or by hand.

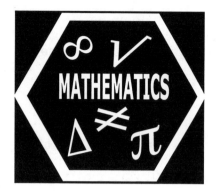

MATHEMATICS

Man Versus Machine

He was coloring a map that he had designed for the counties of England. He wanted the colors to be perfect—complementary—so he was trying various combinations. After a while, he realized that he needed only four colors for his map. Was that always true? He experimented with city maps and still found that he needed only four colors. No matter how complex the map, he could color it with four colors so that no bordering areas were the same color.

Little did British graduate student Francis Gutherie know that his coloring conclusion would lead mathematicians on a 124-year search to solve the Four-Color Theorem. Gutherie wrote about his discovery to his brother Frank, a mathematics student, who in turn brought the discovery to the attention of mathematician Augustus De Morgan (1806–1871). The hunt for a proof to the Four-Color Theorem had begun.

In everyday life, "proof" can be a driver's license, a diploma, or even a proof of purchase. In mathematics, a proof is a convincing argument that a particular mathematical relationship is always true. A proof involves more than showing that something is true in a specific case. For example, consider vertical angles—opposite angles formed by two intersecting lines. When proving that vertical angles are congruent, the proof must involve more than simply measuring pairs of vertical angles to show that every pair is congruent. If you used that method, you would need to measure every possible pair of vertical angles—that would be impossible. Instead, the proof must use logical reasoning based on accepted facts about angles to explain why vertical angles must be congruent.

Although no one could find a map that required five colors, no one could prove that only four colors were needed for every possible map. The Four-Color Theorem frustrated mathematicians until 1976. In that year two mathematicians at the University of Illinois, Kenneth Appel and Wolfgang Haken, proved it using a new kind of proof. They used three high-speed computers to test the Four-Color Theorem with every map conceivably possible—this was no easy task. Their computers required 1,200 hours to do all the checking. When the job was done, the Four-Color Theorem was confirmed in every case: No map needed more than four colors. If Appel and Haken had tried to do this without a computer, they would have had to spend thousands of years checking every possibility, similar to checking every pair of vertical angles. Until computers were invented, it wasn't humanly possible to prove a mathematical relationship by examining every possible example. Even today, some traditional mathematicians do not consider this method as a real proof. However, most mathematicians have now come to accept this method, called proof by exhaustion, as a new tool in the search to verify mathematical relationships such as the Four-Color Theorem.

For this activity, use the map of the continental United States shown on page 33. Beginning with any state, try to color the map using only three colors. Color as many adjacent states as possible without using the same color for any bordering states. How many states can you color using only three colors?

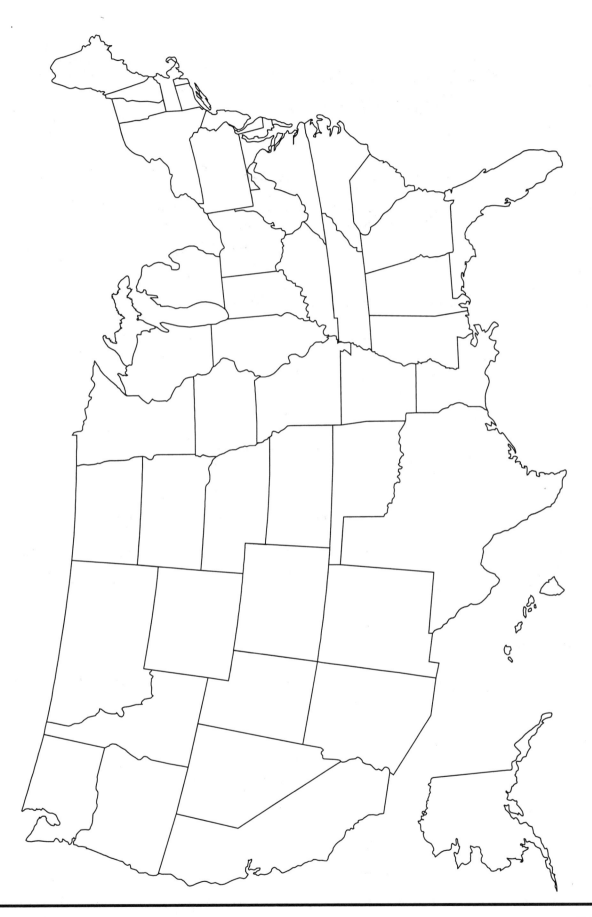

Man Versus Machine
Teacher Page

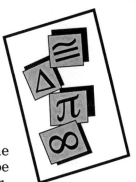

Four colors are needed to color the entire map without using the same color for any bordering states. The number of states that may be colored with only three colors depends on the first state colored. Perhaps propose to students the problem of coloring regions on a torus, a case for which seven colors are needed to ensure that no adjacent regions are the same color. The diagram below shows a torus that has been "unfolded." When the diagram is folded as the arrows show and then the ends are joined, the result is a torus requiring seven colors. (Each of the areas labeled "a" will fold onto each other.)

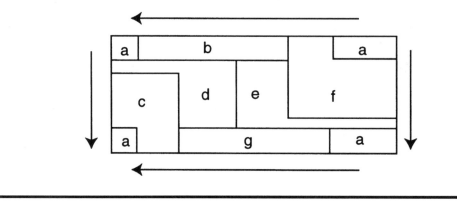

Recently, Neil Robinson, Daniel Sanders, Paul Seymour, and Robin Thomas submitted a more traditional proof of the Four-Color Theorem. Their proof requires working with only 633 configurations rather than the 1,476 configurations used by Appel and Haken. Ultimately, their proof still relies, in part, on a computer-generated algorithm.

Extension

Ask your students to produce a map of only four regions that requires four colors. One such map looks like this:

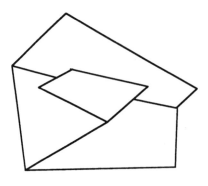

Timing Is Everything

Sometimes, being in the right place at the right time can make all the difference. It certainly did for John Venn (1834–1923). Venn was a little-known mathematician who applied geometric diagrams to the new symbolic algebra of fellow English mathematician George Boole. Venn Diagrams, as they are called, are actually intersecting circles. Venn Diagrams show how members in various groups are related. The only problem is that Venn didn't invent them. Leonhard Euler first used intersecting circles more than a century earlier, and he called them Euler's Circles.

It didn't matter. Venn and his Venn Diagrams became well known because Venn used them with the new algebra. He was in the right place, Great Britain, where George Boole first published this new algebra, at the right time. Venn was the first to apply the simple concept of intersecting circles to symbolic algebra.

The following diagram illustrates how Venn Diagrams may be used to solve problems. For this problem, 12 students are enrolled in geometry, 22 are enrolled in algebra, and 8 are enrolled in both courses. How many students are enrolled in mathematics courses?

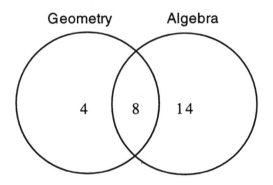

The circles represent students enrolled in each of the two courses of geometry and algebra. The overlapping section represents the students who are taking both courses. A total of 26 students (4 + 8 + 14) are enrolled in mathematics courses.

For this activity, use the Venn Diagram shown below to solve the following problem:

21 students play field hockey

23 students play soccer

12 students play both sports

How many students are participating in these fall sports?

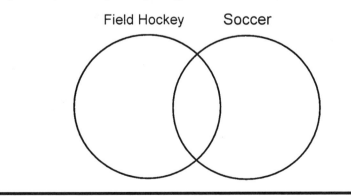

Timing Is Everything
Teacher Page

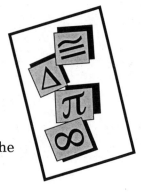

For the student activity, a total of 32 students participate in the sports of field hockey and soccer.

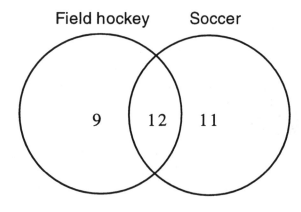

John Venn was another in a long line of mathematicians who were also clergymen. Venn studied mathematics at Cambridge University, but within two years of graduating, he was installed as a priest for the Church of England. He served as a priest for nearly 25 years, but then returned to Cambridge to teach and write about mathematics and philosophy. He left the priesthood because his analytical mind raised so many questions about what he was teaching that he wanted a change. Although Venn left the priesthood, he remained a devout Anglican all his life.

Upon his return to Cambridge, Venn studied and wrote about logic, philosophy, and empirical proofs of Probability Theory. Regardless, it is for his Venn Diagrams, first used in his book *Symbolic Logic* (1881), that Venn will be forever remembered.

Extension

The Venn Diagram on page 37 is more complex, involving three circles. Have students use it to solve the following problem:

> 25 students belong to the chess club.
>
> 30 students belong to the chorus.
>
> 50 students belong to the drama club.
>
> 12 students belong to both the chess club and the chorus.
>
> 15 students belong to both the chorus and the drama club.
>
> 10 students belong to both the drama club and the chess club.
>
> 9 students belong to all three clubs.

How many students participate in these extracurricular activities?

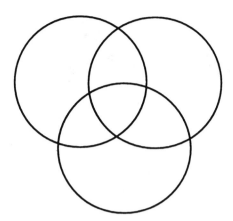

Offer students the hint of first placing in the diagram the number of students who participate in all three activities. Once this group is established in the diagram, the numbers of students in other groups are easier to determine. The total number of students who participate in these clubs is 77.

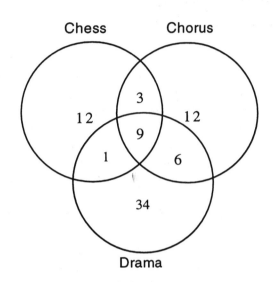

The Number Sifter

Many people earn a nickname or a title when they become adults. Napoleon was known as the Little Corporal; George Washington was known as the Father of His Country; and Elvis Presley was known as the King. Greek mathematician Eratosthenes (c.276–194 B.C.) earned a title as an adult. In fact, he earned two nicknames, Pentathlos and Beta. The word *pentathlos* means "all-around one," and *beta* means "second-rate." These two names seem to contradict each other. How could one person earn both names?

Eratosthenes was certainly an all-around intellect. He wrote with authority on a variety of subjects, including mathematics, history, botany, astronomy, geography, and poetry. He excelled in all of these writings. However, in none of these areas did he make any important or long-lasting discoveries. At least, that's what his critics thought. They believed he was second-rate in anything he did.

Eratosthenes's critics were wrong about his achievements in mathematics. In his honor, one of Eratosthenes's lasting discoveries is called the Sieve of Eratosthenes. It is a method for sifting, or sorting out, prime numbers.

For this activity, you will re-create the Sieve of Eratosthenes. Use the following list of integers from 1 to 150:

1	2	3	4	5	6	7	8	9	10
11	12	13	14	15	16	17	18	19	20
21	22	23	24	25	26	27	28	29	30
31	32	33	34	35	36	37	38	39	40
41	42	43	44	45	46	47	48	49	50
51	52	53	54	55	56	57	58	59	60
61	62	63	64	65	66	67	68	69	70
71	72	73	74	75	76	77	78	79	80
81	82	83	84	85	86	87	88	89	90
91	92	93	94	95	96	97	98	99	100
101	102	103	104	105	106	107	108	109	110
111	112	113	114	115	116	117	118	119	120
121	122	123	124	125	126	127	128	129	130
131	132	133	134	135	136	137	138	139	140
141	142	143	144	145	146	147	148	149	150

1. Cross out the number 1.

2. Circle the number 2 and cross out all multiples of 2.

3. Circle the number 3 and cross out all multiples of 3.

4. Circle the next remaining number in the list (5) and cross out all its multiples.

5. Continue the process until you reach the number 75.

As part of this activity, explain why you can stop at the number 75 and still be certain that you have "sifted" all the prime numbers from the list.

The Number Sifter
Teacher Page

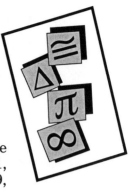

For the student activity, the sieve will find the following prime numbers: 2, 3, 5, 7, 11, 13, 17, 19, 23, 29, 31, 37, 41, 43, 47, 53, 59, 61, 67, 71, 73, 79, 83, 89, 97, 101, 103, 107, 109, 113, 127, 131, 137, 139, 149. Once students reach 75 they may stop because no integers larger than 75 have multiples less than 150.

When he reached middle age, Eratosthenes left his home city of Athens and moved to Alexandria at the invitation of King Ptolemy III. He was to tutor the royal heir in mathematics and history. As befitting a man of his wide-ranging achievements, Eratosthenes was also appointed head librarian of the famous library in Alexandria. Later in life, Eratosthenes suffered from a progressive eye disease. When he could no longer see well enough to read, Eratosthenes ended his life.

Extension

In recent years, the Sieve of Eratosthenes has been improved. One idea to streamline the process is to list only the odd numbers. Because all even numbers (excluding the prime number 2) are multiples of 2, they are composite numbers, or numbers having two or more prime factors. Thus, there is no need to include them in the list of potential primes. Nicomachus of Gerasa wrote in the first century that Eratosthenes was aware of this improvement and used it himself. Similarly, another improvement might be to eliminate multiples of 5 from the list of potential primes.

Ask students to propose ways to improve the Sieve of Eratosthenes. Perhaps suggest improving the sieve by eliminating even numbers, and then ask students to propose another improvement.

The Perfect Child

Would you like to be raised to be the perfect child? Imagine the life you might have if you were expected to be perfect. This was the childhood of Hypatia of Alexandria (370–415), the first known female mathematician. Her father, Theon, tried to raise his only child to be perfect. Did he succeed? Was Hypatia a perfect child?

Hypatia was born at a time when women stayed at home; only the men went to school, held jobs, and became involved in government. Fortunately for Hypatia, and for the world of mathematics, Theon decided to raise his daughter as he would a son. Hypatia was very young when her mother died, so she spent most of her childhood with only her father. Because Theon was a professor and an administrator at the University of Alexandria, Egypt, Hypatia spent much of her time there while growing up. She attended classes, joined discussions, and studied with her father. Theon was a worthy teacher. He taught Hypatia more than just mathematics; he taught her about the fine arts, science, astronomy, and literature. He also supervised her physical fitness, through a training program of swimming, rowing, and aerobic exercises. When she was a teenager, Hypatia traveled to Athens, Greece, and attended the school taught by Greek biographer Plutarch.

When Hypatia returned to Alexandria, she joined the university as a teacher. By all reports, she was an outstanding teacher and lecturer in both mathematics and literature. She invented the astrolabe to help sailors navigate by the stars, and developed a new method to distill water. Topics of her writings include algebraic equations and conic sections. In all her writings, her explanations are clear and concise.

Unfortunately, Hypatia's fame as an outstanding teacher also spelled her doom. At the same time that she was teaching in Alexandria, a small cult of religious fanatics were trying to recruit new members. It was a difficult task because many of the potential recruits were joining the University of Alexandria to listen to Hypatia. Frustrations grew, and so Cyril, the patriarch/archbishop of Alexandria and the cult's leader, held a meeting to discuss what to do about Hypatia. By the end of the meeting, the members were so angry about Hypatia that they were capable of anything to get rid of her. Just as the meeting adjourned, who should be riding past in her chariot? Hypatia. The cult members pulled her from her chariot and tortured her to death.

Was Hypatia a perfect child? Probably not, but she became famous for her teaching, her writing, and her beauty. Certainly her father was proud of his "perfect child."

One of the problems that Hypatia wrote about is the following:

> Find an integer that is the sum of two squares and whose square is also the sum of two squares.

This problem is typical of the algebra problems that the ancient Greek mathematicians studied. It has more than one answer. In fact, there are three numbers less than 20 that solve the problem. For this activity, find the three numbers.

The Perfect Child
Teacher Page

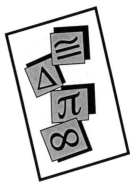

Hypatia discovered that prime numbers of the form $4n + 1$ will always solve the problem:

$$4(1) + 1 = 5 = 1^2 + 2^2 \qquad 5^2 = 3^2 + 4^2$$
$$4(4) + 1 = 17 = 1^2 + 4^2 \qquad 17^2 = 8^2 + 15^2$$

The formula does not yield all the answers to the problem, the third solution for which is 10:

$$10 = 1^2 + 3^2 \qquad 10^2 = 6^2 + 8^2$$

Hypatia's fate was more a case of poor timing than anything else. The small group of fanatical Christians were concerned with Hypatia's popularity because she was a pagan and, further so, because she associated with the Jews of Alexandria. However, the Christians weren't terrorists or assassins. Had Hypatia passed their location a mere five minutes earlier, it is unlikely she would have died at their hands.

Some have suggested that Hypatia should be known as the Mother of Algebra because her work helped preserve and extend what the Father of Algebra, Diophantus, wrote years earlier. Some of Diophantus's work would have been lost without Hypatia's writings and commentaries about it.

For centuries after Hypatia, few women followed her footsteps into mathematics. The reasons are many and varied, ranging from lack of opportunity for women to outright prejudice against them. Those who did succeed sometimes did so because of unusual circumstances. The great Russian mathematician Sonya Kovalevsky (1850–1891) might never have become a mathematician had it not been for her bedroom wallpaper. When Sonya was a young girl, she and her family moved into a large house much in need of repairs. The money for repairs, though, was spent before Sonya's bedroom could be wallpapered. The walls needed some sort of covering, so the family papered them with her father's university notes. Every night for many years, Sonya fell asleep looking at the notes on her wall. It was some years later, in her first calculus course, that the notes on the wall came to mind. To Sonya, understanding the work seemed so easy, as if she had seen it all before. She had. The notes on the wall were her father's calculus notes! Her immediate success in mathematics made it possible for her to advance quickly to higher mathematics classes before any prejudice against women could prevent her from doing so.

From *Famous Problems and Their Mathematicians.* © 1999 Art Johnson. Teacher Ideas Press. (800) 237-6124.

Extension

One of the topics Kovalevsky wrote about was the rotation of a solid body about a fixed point, work for which she won the Prix Bordin, an international mathematics award. The mathematics of Kovalevsky's work is beyond the understanding of most high school students. However, most students are able to rotate plane figures about an axis, an elementary version of Kovalevsky's studies. Have students describe the solids that result when the plane figures shown below are rotated about an axis.

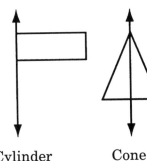 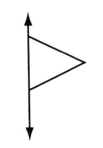 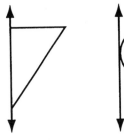 

Cylinder   Cone   Two cones sharing a base   Cone   Torus

The Blockhead

What do you think of the nickname Fibonacci, which means "Blockhead"? Would you pick this nickname for yourself? Of course not, but Leonardo of Pisa (c.1175–1228) did when he published his first mathematics book. Why would he use a nickname? Why the nickname Blockhead? The reason concerns the first sentence of *Liber Abaci*, the book Leonardo published in 1202.

In *Liber Abaci*, Leonardo of Pisa, or Fibonacci, to use his nickname, began the first chapter with: "There are nine figures of the Indian 1 2 3 4 5 6 7 8 9. With these nine figures and the symbol 0, which in Arabic is called *zephirum*, any number can be written as will be demonstrated below." The sentence marks one of the first times any European mathematician described zero. Although the concept of zero originated centuries earlier in India and the Middle East, it was relatively unknown in the Europe of Fibonacci's time. This idea of using zero along with the other nine digits of the Hindu-Arabic numeral system led to his nickname.

You have probably written and read numbers represented with Roman numerals. If you have, you know how much easier zero and the nine digits of the Hindu-Arabic numeral system are to use. Eight hundred years ago, people weren't so sure. They were suspicious of anything that came from the non-Christian East. In 1298, the city council of Florence, Italy, a large center of commerce, banned the use of zero entirely. Why? Because the new Hindu-Arabic numerals were too easy to forge. For example, 10 could be changed to 110, or 101, or even 16 with a single pen stroke. Fibonacci's critics called him a blockhead because he argued in favor of the new numeral system. To answer his critics, Fibonacci adopted the nickname they gave him to show what even a blockhead could do with the superior Hindu-Arabic numerals.

One of the problems in *Liber Abaci* is known as the Rabbit Problem. It is one of the most famous problems in the history of mathematics. For this activity, design a chart to record the values you find when solving the problem.

> A man put a pair of rabbits in a particular place entirely surrounded by a wall. How many pairs of rabbits will be produced from that pair in a year if the nature of these rabbits is such that each month, each pair bears a new pair that becomes productive from the second month onward?

Hint: Be sure to count pairs of rabbits, and not individual rabbits. Look for a pattern in the progressive total number of rabbit pairs for each month.

The Blockhead
Teacher Page

The solution to the student activity is the famous Fibonacci Sequence:

$$1, 1, 2, 3, 5, 8, 13, 21, \ldots$$

In this sequence, each term is the sum of the previous two terms ($1 + 1 = 2, 2 + 1 = 3, 3 + 2 = 5, 5 + 3 = 8, 8 + 5 = 13, 13 + 8 = 21, \ldots$). As the series continues, the ratio of one term to the next consecutive term approaches the Golden Ratio:

$$\frac{\sqrt{5}-1}{2} \approx .618$$

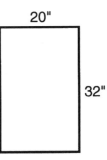

This ratio has been used for centuries by artists. In ancient Egypt, artisans were commanded by the pharaohs to include the Golden Ratio in their work. The Golden Ratio appears in nature in such diverse places as the curve of a seashell, the nodules on a pineapple, and the curve of a ram's horn. The Golden Ratio is a standard feature of many modern designs, from postcards and credit cards to posters and light-switch plates.

Extension

Fibonacci included the following problem in *Liber Abaci*:

> There are seven old women on the road to Rome. Each woman has seven mules; each mule carries seven sacks; each sack contains seven loaves; with each loaf are seven knives; and each knife is in seven sheaths. Women, mules, sacks, loaves, knives, and sheaths—how many are there in all on the road to Rome?

This problem is reminiscent of an English nursery rhyme:

> As I was going to St. Ives,
> I met a man with seven wives;
> Every wife had seven sacks;
> Every sack had seven cats;
> Every cat had seven kits.
> Kits, cats, sacks, and wives,
> How many were going to St. Ives?

The Blockhead Teacher Page continues on page 46.

For the first problem, the solution resembles a set of data from Problem 79 in the Rhind Papyrus, a collection of problems from ancient Egypt (see "The Unknown Mathematicians," p. 100):

Rhind Papyrus Solution

Houses: 7

Cats: 49

Mice: 343

Heads of wheat: 2,401

Hekat measures: 16,807

Total: 19,607

Fibonacci's Solution

Women: 7

Mules: 49

Sacks: 343

Loaves: 2,401

Knives: 16,807

Sheaths: 117,649

Total: 137,256

The solution to the rhyme is simply 1: the narrator! Present both problems to your students to solve, giving the hint that the problems have different solutions.

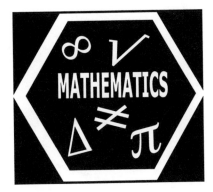

The Man Who Loved Numbers

In 1913, British mathematician G. H. Hardy (1877–1947) received a bulky envelope by mail, full of page after page of equations, with a postmark from India. Hardy didn't know anyone in India. He had received mail from strangers before, but they usually sent incorrect conjectures or confused conclusions about mathematics. This was different. Some of the equations were very familiar, almost elementary, but others were new. Hardy and fellow mathematician John Littlewood (1885–1977) began to examine all the equations. Who was the stranger who sent equations that impressed even Hardy? He was an unknown writer from India, Srinivasa Ayanger Ramanujan (1887–1920).

Although Ramanujan was born to a poor family, he attended public school. When he graduated, he was given a fellowship to the University of Madras. Ramanujan was accepted on the basis of his superior mathematical ability, but he soon left school. He spent all his time doing mathematics and ignored his other subjects. After he dropped out, Ramanujan continued to study mathematics and collect his findings in his notebooks. He tried several times to enter other universities, but his applications were denied. He married in 1909 and began working full-time to support his family. All the while, he continued to advance his mathematical knowledge. He sent his findings to two British mathematicians, but they discarded his notes without even a letter in reply. Finally, Ramanujan wrote to Hardy.

After Hardy had examined Ramanujan's equations, he invited Ramanujan to join him at Cambridge University. Ramanujan traveled to England in 1914. For the next three years, he made extensive advances in mathematics and published 25 papers about his findings. However, the cool, damp British climate was far different from the weather at Ramanujan's home in India, and his health suffered. Eventually, Ramanujan contracted tuberculosis and returned to India, where he died in 1920. When he died, Littlewood said that Ramanujan considered "every natural number as a friend."

On one occasion when Ramanujan was hospitalized in England, Hardy came to visit. It was obvious that Ramanujan was in pain, and Hardy wasn't sure how to begin a conversation with the stranger who had now become his friend. He finally said that he had come to the hospital in taxi number 1,729 and commented, "It seems like a rather dull number, don't you think?" Ramanujan replied, "No, Hardy. It is a very interesting number. It is the smallest number expressible as the sum of two cubes in two different ways."

For this activity, show how 1,729 can be expressed as the sum of two different cubes, in two different ways. In other words, find values for *a*, *b*, *c*, and *d* for the following equation:

$$1{,}729 = a^3 + b^3 = c^3 + d^3$$

Hint: Make a table of cubes to help you in your search.

The Man Who Loved Numbers Teacher Page

The solution to the student activity is:

$$1{,}729 = 1^3 + 12^3 = 9^3 + 10^3$$

The account of Ramanujan in the hospital epitomizes his natural ability with numbers. His genius was such that the mathematics he developed in India was a combination of conjecture and prodigious mental calculation. Regarding his reasoning process, his friend Hardy said, "His ideas as to what constituted a mathematical proof were of the most shadowy descriptions. . . . All his results had been arrived at by a process of mingled argument, intuitions, and induction." Clearly, the concept of formal proof was foreign to him, yet he made contributions to continued fractions, hyperbolic functions, elliptic functions, infinite series, and the analytical theory of numbers.

Ramanujan was a product of his culture. His wife was only nine years old when they married. As a devout Hindu, Ramanajun was a vegetarian, a practice that some feel contributed to his ill health and untimely death. Even after he died, Ramanujan continued to contribute to mathematics. G. N. Watson published 14 papers, each entitled "Theorems Stated by Ramanujan."

Extension

Although Ramanujan's discoveries in mathematics are complex and beyond the understanding of most students, the problem below is one that most students can solve. It involves Armstrong Numbers and it is typical of the problems Ramanujan solved. An Armstrong Number is a number that is equal to the sum of the cubes of its digits ($abc = a^3 + b^3 + c^3$). There are four three-digit Armstrong Numbers. Ask your students to use the table of cubes they made for the student activity to find them:

$$153 = 1^3 + 5^3 + 3^3$$

$$370 = 3^3 + 7^3 + 0^3$$

$$371 = 3^3 + 7^3 + 1^3$$

$$407 = 4^3 + 0^3 + 7^3$$

As a hint, you could tell students that one Armstrong number is between 100 and 200, two of them are between 300 and 400, and one is between 400 and 500.

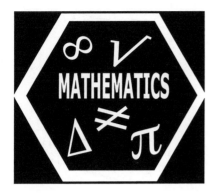

MATHEMATICS

The Search Continues

There have been few discoveries in any field that were still being researched centuries later. French monk and mathematician Marin Mersenne (1588–1648) made one in mathematics that is still being researched today. What did Mersenne discover that inspires research nearly 400 years later?

Mersenne was a Minimite monk who also wrote about mathematics. While serving his religious order at Minims de L'Annociade in Paris from 1619 to 1648, he corresponded with mathematicians and scientists throughout Europe. At the time of his death, Mersenne was maintaining an active correspondence with 70 individuals. Some of his correspondents were Galileo, Descartes, Torricelli, and Roberval. He transmitted ideas and discoveries from one mathematician to another, adding his own ideas and findings. Some historians claim that without Mersenne, the development of mathematics would have been held back for 100 years.

What discovery of Mersenne's is still the subject of research today? Mersenne Primes. A prime number is a number that is divisible only by itself and 1. In *Cogitata Physico-Mathematica*, published in 1644, Mersenne claimed that numbers of the form $2^n - 1$ are prime numbers. Any number in this form is called a Mersenne Prime. For example, the third Mersenne Prime ($n = 3$) is $2^3 - 1 = 8 - 1 = 7$, which is a prime number. Not all Mersenne Primes are prime numbers, but many are. Mersenne Primes have led to current research to discover the largest prime number. As of 1999, Nayan Hajratwala was credited with finding the largest Mersenne Prime: $2^{6,972,593} - 1$. It has 2,098,960 digits; if printed in the format for a typical paperback book, the number would fill over 1,050 pages!

For this activity, examine the first 10 Mersenne Primes (that is, all the numbers in the form $2^n - 1$ for values of n from 1 to 10) to determine a pattern for finding prime numbers using Mersenne's formula: $2^n - 1$. Look for a relationship between the value of n and whether the resulting number is a prime number.

The Search Continues
Teacher Page

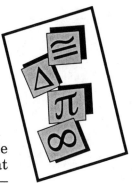

Based on the first 10 Mersenne Primes, students should conclude that Mersenne Primes are generated by $2^n - 1$ only for values of n that are themselves prime. Thus, the fourth Mersenne Prime ($n = 4$) is $2^4 - 1 = 16 - 1 = 15$, a number that is not prime but composite. However, the stipulation about n being a prime number is not entirely correct. For example, $2^{29} - 1$ is not a prime number even though 29 is a prime number. Thus, the current research to find the largest prime number using Mersenne Primes is not simply a matter of computing $2^n - 1$ for large values of n because the resulting number must be carefully checked to determine if it is, in fact, a prime number.

The search for the largest prime has a long history, which began shortly after Mersenne's death. The largest prime found by longhand method was $2^{127} - 1$, discovered in 1876 by John Lucas:

$$170,141,183,460,469,231,731,687,303,715,884,105,727$$

Since then, increasingly larger primes have been discovered using calculators and, now, high-speed computers. The first million-digit Mersenne Prime will soon be discovered.

It is interesting that Mersenne is so well remembered for what was essentially a simple conjecture about prime numbers. Mersenne also made discoveries about the length and periodicity of a pendulum, and about vibrating strings, optics, and acoustics. His greatest contribution to mathematics, though, was probably the weekly sessions he held at his residence from about 1635 to his death in 1648. His guest list reads like a Who's Who of mathematicians and scientists, including René Descartes, whom Mersenne met when they were both students at La Fleche in France; Fermat; Pascal; Roberval; Hobbes; and Battista. It was at one of these gatherings that a young Blaise Pascal met René Descartes. These weekly meetings are considered the beginning of what became the famous Academy Royale des Sciences.

Extension

The study of prime numbers was begun by Euclid because prime numbers are related to perfect numbers, which were highly esteemed by the ancient Greeks. A perfect number is a number whose divisors (including the divisor 1 but not itself as a divisor) sum to the number itself. To find a perfect number using a Mersenne Prime, multiply the Mersenne Prime by 2^{n-1}. The first two perfect numbers are $(2^2 - 1)2^1 = 6 = 1 + 2 + 3$, and $(2^3 - 1)2^2 = 28 = 1 + 2 + 4 + 7 + 14$. Have students examine the integers from 1 to 30 to find these two perfect numbers. They might also try to show that 496, or $(2^5 - 1)2^4$, and 8,128, or $(2^7 - 1)2^6$, are perfect numbers:

$$496 = 1 + 2 + 4 + 8 + 16 + 31 + 62 + 124 + 248$$

$$8,128 = 1 + 2 + 4 + 8 + 16 + 32 + 64 + 127 + 254 + 508 + 1,016 + 2,032 + 4,064$$

These first four perfect numbers were known to the ancient Greek and Syrian mathematicians. Both Theon of Smyrna (c.130) and Nicomachus of Gerasa (c.60–c.120) cite them in their writings. Interestingly, they were also known to tenth-century Benedictine nun Hrotsvitha. She included them in a play she wrote at Gandersheim Abbey in Saxony. The largest perfect number found as of 1999 (using the largest known Mersenne Prime) is $(2^{6,972,592} - 1)2^{6,972,593} - 1$. It has 4,197,919 digits.

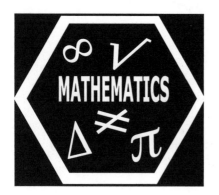

A Difficult Childhood

Nicolo Fortuna (c.1500–1557) was born in Italy, at a time when French and Italian troops seemed to be fighting one continuous battle near his hometown. His mother died when he was very young. When he was only 12, he saw his father killed during an attack by foreign troops. During this attack, young Nicolo was struck by a sword across the mouth and jaw. The wound left a large scar, which Nicolo hid with a lush beard as he grew older. The injury also caused a lifelong stutter so severe that he became known as Nicolo Tartaglia—Nicolo the Stammerer.

With such a difficult childhood, one might hope that Tartaglia found happiness in adult life. For a while, he did. Tartaglia eventually became a well-known mathematician, constantly in demand for his ability to use mathematics to help local nobles' troops accurately aim their cannons. He also discovered a method for solving cubic equations.

One of the problems Tartaglia wrote about is called the River-Crossing Problem, a problem found in many cultures, in various forms (see "The Most Learned Scholar of His Time," p. 116). One version of the River-Crossing Problem is the following:

> A merchant needs to cross a river with his goose, a basket of corn, and a fox. The boat the merchant wishes to take will hold only the merchant and one other thing.
>
> If the goose is left alone with the corn, the goose will eat the corn.
>
> If the fox is left alone with the goose, the fox will eat the goose.
>
> How can the merchant get them all across? How many trips must he take?

For this activity, make a diagram to show the trips the merchant must take to get everything across.

A Difficult Childhood
Teacher Page

To represent the diagram for the student activity, let F represent the fox, C the corn, G the goose, M the merchant, and ∣ the river. For convenience, assume that the river is oriented north to south, and that the merchant must cross from the west bank, the left side of ∣, to the east bank, the right side of ∣.

1. All are on the west bank of the river. $F\ C\ G\ M$ ∣

2. The merchant takes the goose across the river to the east bank: $F\ C$ ∣ $G\ M$

3. He returns alone to the west bank: $F\ C\ M$ ∣ G

4. The merchant takes the fox across the river to the east bank: C ∣ $G\ F\ M$

5. He returns to the west bank with the goose: $C\ G\ M$ ∣ F

6. The merchant leaves the goose on the west bank and takes the corn across the river to the east bank: G ∣ $F\ C\ M$

7. He returns alone to the west bank: $G\ M$ ∣ $F\ C$

8. The merchant takes the goose across to the east bank: ∣ $F\ C\ G\ M$

Although Tartaglia found happiness for a while, his later life would become nearly as tragic as his youth. He became an accomplished mathematician when he matured, winning his share of mathematics competitions against the court mathematicians of other nobles. Eventually, Tartaglia solved an equation of the type $x^3 + px = q$, which no one else could solve. This gave Tartaglia an advantage over all others, and he began to win every competition he entered.

News of Tartaglia's discovery reached another mathematician of the times, Girolamo Cardano (1501–1576), an accomplished mathematician, physician (possibly the most famous in all of Europe), writer, and more. Cardano was a talented storyteller and well traveled, but he had a dark side as well. He was a womanizer, drank heavily, and abused his children—and now, he intended to discover the secret of Tartaglia's solution.

Cardano wrote to Tartaglia, asking for the secret, but Tartaglia refused to reveal it because he was planning to write a book about his algebra discoveries. Cardano traveled to meet Tartaglia in person to ask him for the secret to the solution. By using all his talents, Cardano persuaded Tartaglia into revealing his well-kept secret. In return, Cardano vowed never to reveal it to anyone else.

A Difficult Childhood Teacher Page continues on page 54.

Soon after the meeting, Tartaglia's worst fears were realized. Cardano published *Ars Magna* (1545), the most outstanding mathematics book of the century. With the publication came fame and fortune for Cardano. Although Cardano did honor Tartaglia for the solution of the cubic equation in three separate footnotes, the book was Cardano's, and the credit for the solution of a cubic equation also went to Cardano. Tartaglia spent the rest of his life trying to win what was rightfully his, but to no avail. He never made another discovery to equal his solution of the cubic equation.

Cardano lived nearly 20 years after Tartaglia died, enjoying wealth and fame from *Ars Magna*. His life eventually came to an untimely end, though. In addition to all his other pursuits, Cardano was an astrologer. He had predicted his own death—September 21, 1576. When the date arrived, Cardano was still in good health, and the circumstances of his life didn't suggest an imminent death. Still, he determined that there was no mistake in his calculations. To ensure the accuracy of his prediction, Cardano committed suicide!

Extension

Tartaglia's version of the River-Crossing Problem is more complicated than the popular version in the student activity. The following is a translation of the problem as Tartaglia wrote it:

> Three newlyweds come to a riverbank where a small boat is to take them across, but the boat can hold only two people at a time. Each husband is the jealous type and very protective of his beautiful wife. In order to keep things peaceful, they decide that no woman is to be left with a man unless her husband is present. How can the couples get to the other side?

Have students act out this problem, recording each stage of their solution. One solution is as follows: Let Ah and Aw represent the first couple (the husband and wife, respectively), Bh and Bw the second couple, Ch and Cw the third couple, and | the river. For convenience, assume that the river is oriented north to south, and that the couples must cross from the west bank, the left side of |, to the east bank, the right side of |.

1.	All are on the west bank of the river.	$Ah\ Aw\ Bh\ Bw\ Ch\ Cw$	
2.	Couple A cross the river.	$Bh\ Bw\ Ch\ Cw$	$Ah\ Aw$
3.	Husband A returns.	$Ah\ Bh\ Bw\ Ch\ Cw$	Aw
4.	Couple B cross the river.	$Ah\ Ch\ Cw$	$Aw\ Bh\ Bw$
5.	Husband B returns.	$Ah\ Bh\ Ch\ Cw$	$Aw\ Bw$
6.	Husbands A and B cross the river.	$Ch\ Cw$	$Ah\ Aw\ Bh\ Bw$
7.	Wife A returns.	$Aw\ Ch\ Cw$	$Ah\ Bh\ Bw$
8.	Couple C cross the river.	Aw	$Ah\ Bh\ Bw\ Ch\ Cw$
9.	Wife B returns.	$Aw\ Bw$	$Ah\ Bh\ Ch\ Cw$
10.	Wives A and B cross the river.		$Ah\ Aw\ Bh\ Bw\ Ch\ Cw$

The Misunderstood Mathematician

Sometimes people become famous because someone else writes about them. For example, we know about Greek philosopher Socrates because one of his students, Plato, wrote about him. It was just the opposite for French mathematician Nicholas Chuquet (1448–1500). In 1484, Chuquet published *Triparty en la Science des Nombres*, a book that advanced the development of modern algebra and also covered commercial arithmetic and practical geometry. However, Chuquet's book was handwritten in manuscript form. Because it was not formally printed and published, *Triparty* was not widely read. A student of Chuquet's, Estienne de La Roche (1480–1520), printed *L'Arismetique* in 1520 to help explain and popularize what Chuquet had written. La Roche's book had the opposite effect. Not only had he misunderstood some of Chuquet's book, but he also excluded some of the more interesting sections because he thought they would be too confusing. The result was that most people considered Chuquet to be a second-rate mathematician who wrote a third-rate book. It was not until 1880, when Aristide Marre produced a printed copy of the *Triparty*, that Chuquet began receiving recognition as the outstanding mathematician of his day.

The following problem appeared in Chuquet's book:

> A man spent 1/3 of his money and lost 2/3 of the remainder. He then had 12 pieces. How many pieces had he at first?

For this activity, try to solve the problem using diagrams. Assume that each piece of money has equal value.

The Misunderstood
Mathematician Teacher Page

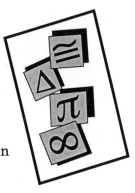

The solution to the student problem is 54 pieces, solving for x in the following equation:

$$\frac{2}{3}x - \frac{2}{3}(\frac{2}{3}x) = 12; \quad x = 54$$

Triparty was a milestone in the history of mathematics. It contained much about the language and mathematics of the marketplace, matters of great importance to the merchant families of the Renaissance. It was full of problems involving trade, finances, and related commercial topics. It also reflected the advances being made in mathematics at that time.

In *Triparty*, Chuquet explained his system for naming powers of 10, coining the terms *billion, trillion, quadrillion*, and so forth: "The first dot indicates million, the second dot billion, the third dot trillion, the fourth dot quadrillion . . . and so on as far as one may wish to go." Chuquet also began the shift of algebra from the geometric foundation of the ancient Greeks to the analytical approaches of the Arabic mathematicians by replacing the terms *square root* and *cube root* with the terms *second root* and *third root*. Chuquet thus anticipated equations with fourth and fifth roots, which were analyzed in the next century. Chuquet also described negative numbers in *Triparty*; however, he described them as "absurd quantities." Another 100 years would pass before negative numbers would be accepted as legitimate by the mathematics community.

Extension

When Chuquet wrote *Triparty*, modern mathematics notation was only in the beginning of its development. For the next 200 years, a wide range of mathematicians contributed to the symbols that are used today. Ask students to try to factor and solve the following quadratic equation using Chuquet's notation:

	Equation	Solution
Modern Notation	$3x^2 + 3x = 27$	$x = -3, 4.5$
Chuquet's Notation	3^2 p3^1 égault 27	Res égault 3

(*Res* is Latin for "thing.")

A Victim of the Times

Most mathematicians did more than teach and write about mathematics. They raised families, held jobs, and even fought in wars. Sometimes, mathematicians became tragic victims of events around them. That's what happened to Georg Alexander Pick (1859–1943). Pick was born in Vienna, Austria. He lived a quiet life, teaching and writing about mathematics until the 1930s, when Austria became engulfed by the Third Reich of Nazi Germany. Although Pick was by then far too old to serve in the armed forces, he had a more serious reason to be worried: He was Jewish. Eventually, Pick came to the attention of the Nazi authorities, and he was sent to the Theresienstadt concentration camp. He died there about 1943.

Georg Pick is known for Pick's Theorem, his method for finding the area of polygons on a square-unit grid of points (each vertex must occur at a point on the grid), such as for the following polygon:

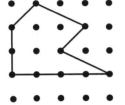

You could find the square-unit area of this polygon by cutting it into smaller polygons and finding the areas of those polygons. Or, you could use Pick's Theorem:

$$\text{Area} = i + \frac{1}{2}b - 1$$

In this formula, i represents the number of grid points inside the polygon, and b represents the number of grid points on the boundary of the polygon. For this polygon, $i = 3$ and $b = 10$:

$$\text{Area} = 3 + \frac{1}{2}(10) - 1 = 7 \text{ square units}$$

For this activity, use Pick's Theorem to find the square-unit area of the polygon below. Then, draw a polygon of your own and ask a classmate to find its area.

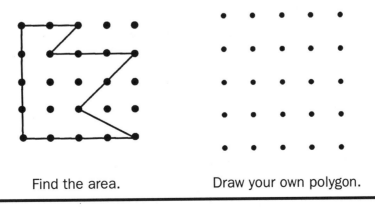

Find the area.   Draw your own polygon.

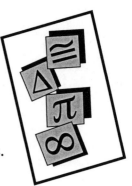

A Victim of the Times
Teacher Page

For the student activity, the area of the polygon is 10.5 square units.

Pick first published his theorem in 1899 in *Geometrisches zur Zahlenlehre*, but it went unnoticed for decades. It was in 1969, when H. Steinhaus included an article about the theorem in his milestone book, *Mathematical Snapshots*, that Pick's Theorem was made known to the mathematics community at large.

It was unusual for Pick to have been sent to the Theresienstadt concentration camp, which was generally reserved for young children. Why Pick was sent there will never be known. Perhaps because of his advanced age, Pick filled the role of a grandfatherly figure for the children during their last days.

Extension

Present the following two polygons with holes to your students. Have them find the square-unit areas by partitioning each into at least two polygons (thus eliminating the hole) and finding the square-unit areas of the partitioned polygons using Pick's Theorem. Ask students to conjecture whether Pick's Theorem is true for polygons with holes (it is). Have them use the theorem again to find the square-unit areas, but without partitioning the polygons, and compare results.

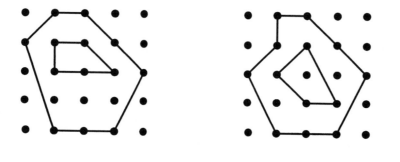

$$\text{Area} = 3 + \frac{1}{2}(13) - 1 = 8.5 \qquad \text{Area} = 2 + \frac{1}{2}(13) - 1 = 7.5$$

Numbers with Personality

Have you ever thought of numbers as having a personality? Maybe you've looked at complex fractions and thought they looked a bit mean, but how about "younger," "older," "beautiful," "excellent," or "ordinary and ugly"? This is how Nicomachus of Gerasa (c.60–120) thought of numbers. His whole philosophy of life revolved around numbers. Nicomachus was a Syrian mathematician who spent most of his life near Jerusalem, far from Rome or Alexandria, the learning centers of the ancient world.

Many of Nicomachus's writings have been lost. However, his major work, *Introductio Arithmetica*, has survived. As the title suggests, *Introductio Arithmetica* was an introduction to arithmetic. It was the first arithmetic book ever written. All previous mathematics books were about geometry or applications of geometry. In his book, Nicomachus described various numbers according to their properties. He called a number that was equal to the sum of its divisors (including the divisor 1 but not itself as a divisor) "perfect," or "excellent." For example, the number 28 is a perfect number ($28 = 1 + 2 + 4 + 7 + 14$). He considered all other numbers to be "ugly."

Nicomachus also named numbers as being "abundant" or "deficient." A number is an abundant number if the sum of its divisors is greater than the number itself. For example, the number 12 is an abundant number ($1 + 2 + 3 + 4 + 6 > 12$). A number is a deficient number if the sum of its divisors is less than the number itself. For example, the number 8 is a deficient number ($1 + 2 + 4 < 8$).

There are nine abundant numbers less than 50. One of them is 12. For this activity, find the other eight abundant numbers less than 50. Make a list of them and their divisors.

Numbers with Personality
Teacher Page

The nine abundant numbers less than 50 are 12, 18, 20, 24, 30, 36, 40, 42, and 48.

Introductio Arithmetica was not a mathematics text in the traditional sense. It seems that Nicomachus wrote it as a handbook for the general population. He even included a multiplication table for the integers 1 to 10. Nicomachus also presented many theorems and number relationships, but without proofs. Instead, he showed many examples to demonstrate his theorems. For instance, he showed that consecutive series of sums of consecutive odd integers were perfect cubes:

$$1 = 1^3$$
$$3 + 5 = 2^3$$
$$7 + 9 + 11 = 3^3$$
$$13 + 15 + 17 + 19 = 4^3$$
$$\vdots$$

It is likely that his philosophical outlook that numbers have personalities was reflected in how he wrote the book. It was a very popular book for which he became well known in the ancient world.

Nicomachus also wrote extensively in *Introductio Arithmetica* about figurate or polygonal numbers, which are numbers that can be represented by geometric figures (see "Less Is More," p. 66). In addition to writing about polygonal numbers (numbers represented by polygons), he wrote about polyhedral numbers. A polyhedral number is represented by polyhedrons, such as a triangular pyramid:

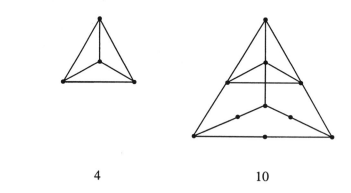

1   4   10

The first six polyhedral numbers for a triangular pyramid and a square pyramid are as follows:

Triangular pyramid: 1, 4, 10, 20, 35, 56

Square pyramid: 1, 5, 14, 30, 55, 91

There is a pattern to each of these series. For the triangular pyramid, each successive number is greater by a successive triangular number (1, 3, 6, 10, 15, 21, ...). For the square pyramid, each successive number is greater by a successive square number (1, 4, 9, 16, 25, 36, ...).

Extension

Demonstrate some polyhedral numbers to students by stacking marbles to form the polyhedron such as the triangular pyramid or by using some other manipulative. Then ask them to determine the first six polyhedral numbers for both the triangular pyramid and the square pyramid by building models or making sketches until they find a pattern to them.

The Greatest "Could-Have-Been" in the History of Mathematics

French mathematician Blaise Pascal (1623–1662) was the greatest could-have-been in the history of mathematics. If Pascal had not abandoned his pursuit of mathematics at age 31, he might have become the greatest mathematician who ever lived. Why did Pascal abandon mathematics?

Even as a boy, Pascal displayed a genius for mathematics. By age 12, young Blaise had proven most of Euclid's geometry himself, with no textbook to guide him. At age 16, he published a booklet, "The Geometry of Conics," that contained a theorem about a hexagon inscribed in conic sections. This discovery so impressed René Descartes, the greatest living French mathematician of that day, that Descartes refused to believe someone so young could have discovered it. By age 18, Pascal had invented the first calculating machine. It could add and subtract numbers using wheels and gears.

When Pascal was 23, his father fell gravely ill. He was cured by two men who had recently converted to a new religion flourishing in France, Jansenism. Eventually, all of Pascal's family, Pascal included, converted to this strict, conservative religion. Soon, Pascal's family brought pressure upon Pascal to abandon the study of mathematics and devote himself to matters of religion and faith. For a time, Pascal resisted, but eventually, he left mathematics behind. Why would he abandon his beloved pursuit, at which he was so successful? The answer concerns an event that happened on November 23, 1654.

On that day, Pascal was riding a horse-and-carriage across the Nevilly Bridge in Paris. Suddenly, the horses bolted and headed for the side of the bridge and the Seine River below it. The horses broke through the railing and plunged to their death in the river, but the carriage became caught on the bridge. Pascal was saved from a watery death. He believed this event to be evidence of God's displeasure with him, and from that day forward, he devoted himself to his religious writings.

One of the discoveries that Pascal is known for is called Pascal's Triangle, a series of rows of numbers with interesting properties. The first few rows of Pascal's Triangle are as follows:

In Pascal's Triangle, the outside numbers of each row are 1's. All other numbers are determined by adding the two numbers above it on either side. For example, in the last row shown above, the boldface 4 is determined by adding the boldface 1 and 3 in the row above it. Similarly, the 6 in the last row is determined by adding the two 3's in the row above it.

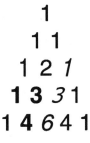

For this activity, copy the rows of Pascal's Triangle shown above and complete the following tasks:

1. Write four more rows for the triangle.

2. The sum of the numbers in each row of the triangle form a pattern. Find the pattern and use it to determine the sum of the numbers that will appear in row 20.

3. The numbers on the diagonal beginning 1, 3, 6, ... (shown in italic) form a pattern. Find the pattern and use it to determine the number that will appear on the same diagonal in row 10.

The Greatest "Could-Have-Been" in the History of Mathematics
Teacher Page

The complete Pascal's Triangle for the student activity is as follows:

```
                  1
                1   1
              1   2   1
            1   3   3   1
          1   4   6   4   1
        1  5  10  10   5   1
      1  6  15  20  15   6   1
    1  7  21  35  35  21   7   1
  1  8  28  56  70  56  28   8   1
```

The sum of the numbers in row n is 2^{n-1}. Thus, the sum of the numbers in row 20 is: $2^{20-1} = 2^{19} = 524{,}288$. The numbers on the selected diagonal are the triangular numbers—successive sums of the natural numbers ($1, 1 + 2 = 3, 1 + 2 + 3 = 6, \ldots$) (see "Less Is More," p. 66).

Pascal's Triangle shows many other patterns, including the coefficients for a binomial expansion $(a + b)^n$. For the exponent n, the coefficients for the expansion are contained in row $n + 1$ of Pascal's Triangle. For example, when $n = 2$, the coefficients $(1, 2, 1)$ are found in row 3: $(a + b)^2 = a^2 + 2ab + b^2$; when $n = 3$, the coefficients $(1, 3, 3, 1)$ are found in row 4: $(a + b)^3 = a^3 + 3a^2b + 3ab^2 + b^3$; and so forth.

Pascal was not the first to discover the triangle that bears his name. Several other mathematicians wrote about it. In tenth-century India, a writer named Halayudha called it the *meruprastara*. In *The Precious Mirror of the Fair Elements* (1303), Chinese mathematician Chu Shih-chieh illustrated the same triangle. German mathematician Michael Stifel wrote about this triangle in *Arithmetica Integra* (1544).

Despite his brush with death, Pascal did not completely abandon mathematics. He returned to it one last time. One day, several years after he had turned to matters of faith, Pascal suffered a severe toothache. In the midst of his pain, Pascal's mind drifted to mathematics and a curve known as the cycloid. While Pascal was thinking about this curve, the toothache disappeared. Believing this to be evidence of divine approval, Pascal happily spent a week analyzing the cycloid. At the end of that week, however, he again abandoned mathematics, this time forever.

In addition to his discoveries in geometry and number theory, Pascal made discoveries in the areas of barometric pressure and the flow of liquids. Pascal is also known as a co-founder of Probability Theory with Pierre de Fermat. Pascal began the study of probability when a friend, Antoine Gombard, the Chevalier De Mere, asked him for help in learning how to gamble more successfully. Gombard explained to Pascal that if he knew how to base his wagers on probable outcomes, he would win more money. Pascal began to think about various games of chance and enlisted Fermat's help in developing a new field of mathematics—Probability Theory.

Extension

The table below is for listing the 36 possible results when rolling a pair of dice. Have students complete the table, and then ask them to use their data to determine the probability of rolling a 6, 7, or 8.

+	1	2	3	4	5	6
1						
2					7	
3						
4		6				
5						
6						

Out of the 36 possible outcomes, 16 are a 6, 7, or 8. Thus, the probability of rolling one of these numbers is 16/36, or 44.4%.

Less Is More

It was a very unusual diary. It covered nearly 20 years. How many pages do you suppose it contained? Think again: It contained only 19 pages! You might be thinking that it couldn't have been much of a diary, but in this case, the diary belonged to Carl Friedrich Gauss (1777–1855), a brilliant German mathematician. Gauss didn't write about everyday events in his diary, like most people. Instead, he recorded his mathematics, ideas and discoveries. Another reason for the diary being so brief is that Gauss recorded an idea only if it was perfectly formed. Even then, he used a minimum number of words. One of his entries (out of 145) was this:

Eureka (num) $= \Delta + \Delta + \Delta$

What Gauss meant by this note is that every positive integer can be expressed by three or fewer triangular numbers. Triangular numbers are successive sums of the natural numbers (1, 1 + 2 = 3, 1 + 2 + 3 = 6, ...) and take the form of triangles when represented with points:

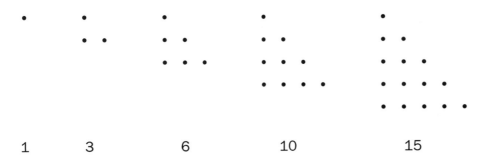

| 1 | 3 | 6 | 10 | 15 |

For this activity, show that Gauss's discovery is true. For example, 28 is the sum of three triangular numbers: 15 + 10 + 3. Select three integers between 50 and 100 and represent each number as the sum of three or fewer triangular numbers. (Hint: Make a list of triangular numbers less than 100.)

Less Is More
Teacher Page

The first entry in Gauss's diary was made on March 30, 1796, when Gauss was only 19. In this entry, Gauss noted that he had proven that a 17-sided polygon could be constructed using the classical construction tools of a compass and straightedge. This was the first advance in constructions since the time of the ancient Greek mathematicians. Gauss was so thrilled with this discovery that he decided to devote himself to the study of mathematics for the rest of his life. He first published his discovery in June 1796 in *Intelligenzblattg der Allegmeiner Literaturzeitung*. Soon after, in 1801, Gauss published the first of several masterworks, *Disquisitions Arithmeticae*. In *Disquisitions*, Gauss proved that the all regular polygons that had a number of sides equal to a Fermat Prime could be constructed.

Fermat Primes, named for French mathematician Pierre de Fermat, take the form $2^{2k} + 1$, for integer values of k. As of 1998, five Fermat Primes have been generated from Fermat's formula: 3, 5, 17, 257, and 65,537. Gauss proved that regular polygons with these numbers of sides could be constructed. A mathematician named Hermes actually constructed the polygon for the last Fermat Prime, a colossus with 65,537 sides. It took him 10 years and several boxes of paper to do so.

Gauss himself never constructed the 17-sided polygon; he simply proved that it could be constructed and left the actual construction to others. Gauss was so proud of his accomplishment that he asked for a 17-sided polygon to be inscribed on his headstone. His headstone shows a 17-pointed star, though, because the engraver thought that the 17-sided polygon would look too much like a circle. The engraver clearly underestimated the importance of this polygon to Gauss.

Extension

Have students investigate triangular and other polygonal numbers, such as those shown below. Have students generate tables of values for a series of polygonal numbers and use the data in their tables to find a pattern for determining the nth term of each series.

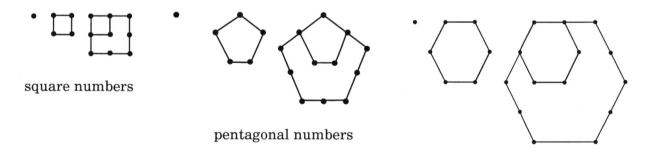

square numbers

pentagonal numbers

hexagonal numbers

Less Is More Teacher Page continues on page 68.

Formulas for the nth terms of the triangular, square, pentagonal, hexagonal, heptagonal, and octagonal series are as follows:

Polygonal Series	nth Term
Triangular 1, 3, 6, ... (1, 1+ 2, 1 + 2 + 3, ...)	$\dfrac{n(n + 1)}{2}$
Square 1, 4, 9, ... (1, 1 + 3, 1 + 3 + 5, ...)	n^2
Pentagonal 1, 5, 12, ... (1, 1 + 4, 1 + 4 + 7, ...)	$\dfrac{n(3n - 1)}{2}$
Hexagonal 1, 6, 15, ... (1, 1 + 5, 1 + 5 + 9, ...)	$\dfrac{n(4n - 2)}{2}$
Heptagonal 1, 7, 18, ... (1, 1 + 6, 1 + 6 + 11, ...)	$\dfrac{n(5n - 3)}{2}$
Octagonal 1, 8, 21, ... (1, 1 + 7, 1 + 7 + 13, ...)	$\dfrac{n(6n - 4)}{2}$

Too Good to Be True

It was an offer he couldn't refuse. Queen Christina of Sweden had even sent an admiral with a fully equipped warship to bring him back to Sweden, if only he would agree. French mathematician and philosopher René Descartes (1596–1650) was impressed. He agreed to move to Sweden and tutor the young queen in mathematics. Descartes was so flattered by this job offer that he forgot to ask about the details. It turned out to be the biggest mistake of his life.

Queen Christina was in the habit of getting up early in the morning and exercising. How early? 5 A.M.! She decided that Descartes could tutor her while she exercised. This was unpleasant enough for Descartes, but the queen also wanted the library windows open so she could breathe fresh air. Poor Descartes; he was not a young man when he took the teaching job. The early morning routine and the cold winter nights of Sweden were too much for him. Soon after beginning to tutor the queen, he caught a cold. Descartes developed pneumonia and, within a week, died.

When Descartes traveled to Sweden, he was known as the greatest mathematician in Europe, a reputation he deserved. Descartes invented analytical geometry and made discoveries in calculus and solid geometry. One of Descartes's well-known findings in solid geometry is called Descartes's Theorem of Angular Deficiency.

In the cube shown below, each angle of the six square faces of the cube measures 90°. At vertex A are three 90° angles. The total of the angle measures at vertex A is $3 \times 90° = 270°$. Because 360° surround any point in a plane, Descartes concluded that the angular deficiency for vertex A (an intersection of three planes) is $360° - 270° = 90°$.

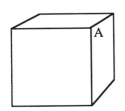

For this activity, find the total angular deficiency for the regular polyhedrons shown below: cube (six square faces, eight vertices), tetrahedron (four triangular faces, four vertices), and octahedron (eight triangular faces, six vertices). To find the total angular deficiency for a polyhedron, find the angular deficiency for each vertex and add together these measurements. Use your results to propose a theorem—the theorem you think Descartes proposed for angular deficiency.

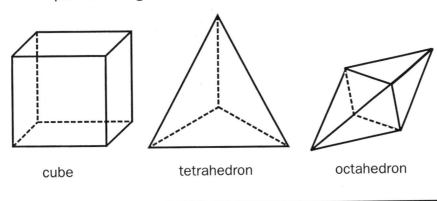

cube   tetrahedron   octahedron

Too Good to Be True
Teacher Page

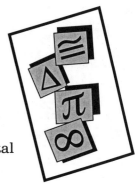

Descartes's Theorem of Angular Deficiency states that the total angular deficiency for any polyhedron is 720°.

Polyhedron	Angular Deficiency, Single Vertex	Number of Vertices	Total Angular Deficiency
Cube	90°	8	90° × 8 = 720°
Tetrahedron	180°	4	180° × 4 = 720°
Octahedron	120°	6	120° × 6 = 720°

Before he left France, René Descartes perhaps suspected what awaited him in Sweden. Based on what he had heard, Descartes described the country as "a land of bears, amongst rocks and ice." Nevertheless, he went, likely because he felt flattered to be tutoring the monarch of a powerful country. Descartes's health had always been frail, for which he compensated by staying in bed each morning until he felt ready to get up. Unfortunately for Descartes, Queen Christina was an early riser, and he could not endure her schedule. As a final indignity, when Descartes's body was returned to France, the official who made the arrangements kept Descartes's right hand as a keepsake of the great mathematician!

Extension

When people think about algebra, they usually envision equations that must be solved for x. Why x? Why not q, or t, or s? The answer concerns René Descartes and a Dutch printer named Jan Maire.

When Descartes wrote his seminal work, *La Géométrie*, he used a scheme of vowels for known quantities and consonants for unknown quantities. For the unknown quantities, Descartes used x, y, and z. During the printing of *La Géométrie*, Maire contacted Descartes about a problem. It seemed he didn't have enough of particular typesetting letters to complete the book as written. He asked Descartes whether specific letters must be used for unknowns. Descartes replied that the specific letters did not matter, as long as vowels were still used for known quantities and consonants for unknown quantities. Maire happened to have more x's than y's or z's, so he used x whenever possible for an unknown quantity. From the publication of *La Géométrie* (1637) forward, x was the letter of choice for a variable in an equation. Thus, solving for x in an equation was more the decision of a printer than a mathematician.

Extension

Despite the fact that Descartes established the standard notation for unknowns, he used a different notation for x^2. He preferred xx to x^2, although he readily used x^3 or x^4. Ask your students to explain why Descartes might have preferred xx to x^2. Some possibilities are that xx requires only a single line in typesetting, and only one font size.

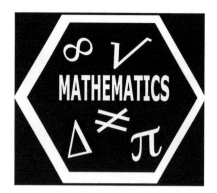

Math in the Mind's Eye

Swiss mathematician Leonhard Euler (1707–1783) found himself in a difficult position: He was going blind. He had already lost his sight in one eye, when he was younger, but now, at the age of 59, he was about to become completely blind. Would this affect Euler's pursuit of mathematics? Would he ever again publish a mathematics article? Would he ever again make a discovery in mathematics? There was no cause for concern. Euler had such a keen mind for mathematics that he continued writing about mathematics and making discoveries. How did he do this? He had the help of two secretaries, who took turns taking notes while Euler dictated. What about all the complex calculations in Euler's mathematics? Simple! Euler performed the calculations in his head.

One of Euler's discoveries is named after him. Euler's Formula concerns the relationships among the numbers of faces, vertices, and edges for various polyhedrons. For this activity, complete the data table below for four polyhedrons:

cube   triangular pyramid   octahedron   square pyramid

Polyhedron	Faces	Vertices	Edges
Cube			
Triangular Pyramid			
Octahedron			
Square Pyramid			

Based on the data, complete Euler's Formula:

Faces + Vertices – Edges = ?

Math in the Mind's Eye
Teacher Page

The completed table for the student activity is as follows:

Polyhedron	Faces	Vertices	Edges
Cube	6	8	12
Triangular Pyramid	4	4	6
Octahedron	8	6	12
Square Pyramid	5	5	8

Euler's Formula is Faces + Vertices − Edges = 2, or $F + V - E = 2$.

After becoming totally blind, Euler continued to work for the remaining 17 years of his life, writing and publishing books and papers about mathematics. The most prolific writer in the history of mathematics, Euler wrote more than 800 books, pamphlets, and articles about a wide range of topics. When he died, his obituary required 56 pages just to list all his publications. It is estimated that Euler alone accounted for nearly one-third of all scientific and mathematics articles published in the eighteenth century.

His ability to perform mathematical calculations in his head was nearly beyond belief. It is said that one day, when his two secretaries were arguing about the 50th decimal place of an infinite series, Euler calculated the elusive digit within seconds.

Extension

Have students investigate whether Euler's Formula is true for concave polyhedrons, including the one shown below and one of their own design.

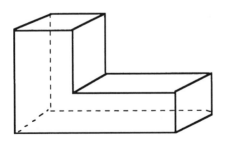

Euler's Formula is valid for this polyhedron (8 + 12 − 18 = 2) and for all polyhedrons, whether convex or concave.

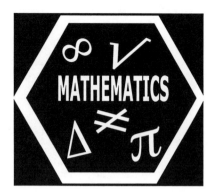

Mathematics Pathways

Irish mathematician William Rowan Hamilton (1805–1865) had worked tirelessly for 15 years on the same idea, but he still hadn't succeeded. Try as he might, he couldn't seem to make the breakthrough he needed. He couldn't find the basic equation to explain the rotation of solids in space. He could almost see it in the back of his mind, but never clearly enough to grasp it.

On the evening of October 16, 1843, Hamilton was walking across the Brogham Bridge over the Royal Canal in Dublin, Ireland, when the equation suddenly came to him. Finally, 15 years of frustration had ended—but wait! Did he have a pencil? He frantically searched all his pockets: No pencil. All he found was a pocketknife. The walk home would take at least 20 minutes. What if he forgot the equation along the way? What then? Another 15 years? In a state of near panic, Hamilton decided to carve the equation into the stonework of the bridge using his pocketknife. As soon as he finished, he hurried home, and then quickly returned with pencil and paper to copy the precious formula.

In 1853, Hamilton revealed his formula to the entire world in *Lectures on Quarternions*. Hamilton invented the term *quarternion* to refer to a group of four numbers that may be used to describe solids rotating in space. The equation that was a crucial part of quarternions, the one that Hamilton carved into the bridge, was $i^2 = j^2 = k^2 = 1$. Quarternions have application to the complex mathematics of the fourth dimension and fractals. The discovery of quarternions earned Hamilton the title of the Greatest Irish Mathematician.

Aside from quarternions, Hamilton also wrote about the mathematics of networks. A network is a series of points joined by segments or paths, such as the network shown here:

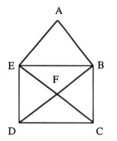

The six points *A*, *B*, *C*, *D*, *E*, and *F* are joined by various segments.

In particular, Hamilton was interested in what is called a Hamilton Circuit, or a Hamilton Walk. A Hamilton Walk is a network that may be traveled in such a manner that each vertex is visited only once along a path that ends at the starting point. The network shown on page 74 is a Hamilton Walk. It has various paths that each visit all six vertices and terminate at the starting vertex. For example, the path *FCBAEDF* is one Hamilton Walk. It begins at vertex *F*, visits each other vertex once, and terminates at the starting point, vertex *F*. (Imagining the paths of a network to be streets, and the vertices to be towns or stores, a Hamilton Walk would essentially be the most efficient solution for a traveling salesperson planning a route: A salesperson would want to begin at home, visit each town or store on the route only once, and end the trip by returning home.)

The network below is more complex. For this activity, try to find a Hamilton Walk for the network. Use vertex labels to describe your walk.

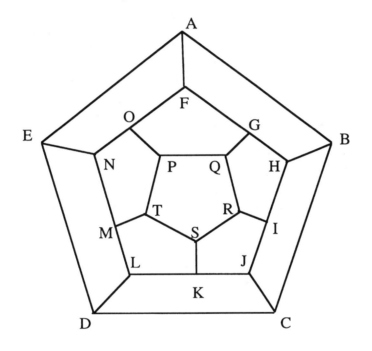

Mathematics Pathways
Teacher Page

One possible Hamilton Walk for the student activity is:

ENMTSRQPOFGHIJKLDCBAE

A footnote to Hamilton's life involves his headstone. Although he was knighted for his achievements in mathematics and died as the most famous Irish mathematician in history, Hamilton's headstone contains a mistake. It notes that Hamilton was born on August 4, 1805. His actual date of birth was August 3, 1805. Why the confusion? Hamilton was born just before midnight, during the last minute of August 3. The headstone engraver erroneously considered the day to be August 4.

The field of networks was actually begun by Swiss mathematician Leonhard Euler (1707–1783), who lived for a time in Konigsberg, Prussia (now Russia). The Pregel River ran through the center of town, forming two islands at the center of the city. In Euler's time, there were seven bridges, joining the islands to each other and to the shore:

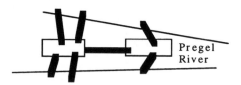

One popular recreation in the Konigsberg of Euler's time was for families to walk across all seven bridges on Sunday afternoons. However, no one could cross each of the seven bridges only once and end where they had begun. Eventually, people concluded that it was impossible. Euler proved that it was impossible. He reduced the bridges and islands of Konigsberg to a simple diagram:

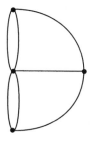

The goal of families in Konigsberg was to travel across every bridge, or network path, and then return to their starting point, without crossing any bridge more than once. Such a network has became known as a Euler Circuit, or Euler Walk. Euler discovered that if a network has an odd vertex (a vertex where an odd number of paths meet), the walk must either begin or end at that vertex. For example, suppose five paths meet at vertex Q. It would be possible to pass through vertex Q twice while traveling between two other vertex points. That would leave a single path to vertex Q that had not been traveled. In order to travel on the last path, it would be necessary to either begin at vertex Q or to end at vertex Q. Thus, for a network to be a Euler Walk, it can have only two odd vertices. The Konigsberg network had four odd vertices, and so was impossible to travel without retracing a path. A Euler Walk describes the route a road inspector would take if the inspector wanted to travel each road once, and only once.

Extension

In 1875, an eighth bridge was added in Konigsberg. Challenge students to find a location for the eighth bridge that creates an open Euler Walk—a walk that crosses each path only once but begins and ends at different vertices. The diagram below shows one of many locations for an eighth bridge that will create an open Euler Walk. However, no matter where the eighth bridge is located, it is still impossible to create a closed Euler Walk, where one ends up at the same place one started.

Today in Konigsberg, only three of the original seven bridges still cross the Pregel River. The townsfolk have had to find a new diversion for Sunday afternoons.

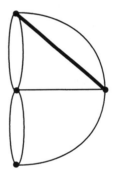

Being Second Doesn't Count

Hungarian mathematician Janos Bolyai (1802–1860) was excited. In a letter to his father (also a mathematician), he wrote, "From nothing I have created another world. I have made such wonderful discoveries that I am myself lost in astonishment." Bolyai had discovered a new kind of geometry, called non-Euclidean geometry, and he was full of enthusiasm because of his discovery. Yet he would suffer heartache because of it. His father suspected what was to come. He wrote to Janos, "For God's sake, please give it up . . . it may take up all your time and deprive you of your health, peace of mind, and happiness in life." Janos should have listened to his father, because he did lose his health, peace of mind, and happiness to non-Euclidean geometry. How could this happen?

Everyone remembers the first person to accomplish something. George Washington was the first president of the United States, Alexander Graham Bell was the first person to speak into a telephone, and Orville Wright was the first person to fly an airplane. The second people to accomplish these things are less well remembered, if at all. The same is true for firsts in mathematics. Throughout history, the same mathematical relationships were discovered by different mathematicians, at different times, independent of one another. The fame and honor usually went to the first to make the discovery.

Bolyai thought he was the first to discover his new geometry when he published it in 1832. He wasn't. First, he learned that Carl Friedrich Gauss, the greatest mathematician of that day, had discovered the same relationships, except Gauss had not published them. Then, Bolyai learned that an obscure Russian mathematician, Nicolai Lobachevsky (1792–1856), had also discovered this geometry. Worse still, Lobachevsky had published his findings in 1826, several years before Bolyai published his findings. This news sent Bolyai into a depression that afflicted him for the rest of his life. His father's warning came true: The new geometry robbed him of all his happiness.

One type of non-Euclidean geometry is geometry on a sphere. The following diagram will help you visualize spherical geometry:

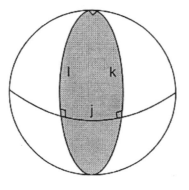

In spherical geometry, a plane is the surface of the sphere. In the diagram, lines *k* and *l* are perpendicular to line *j*, and the intersection of these three lines forms several triangles. The theorems and postulates of spherical geometry are different from the theorems and postulates of Euclidean geometry, the traditional geometry studied in school.

For this activity, use the diagram to help you to rewrite the following familiar theorems and postulates of Euclidean geometry, so that they are true for spherical geometry:

1. Two lines perpendicular to a third line in a plane are parallel.

2. The sum of the angles of a triangle is 180°.

3. Two lines intersect at, at most, one point.

4. A line has infinite length.

Write a theorem or postulate of your own for spherical geometry.

Being Second Doesn't Count
Teacher Page

The rewritten theorems and postulates for the student activity are as follows:

1. Two lines perpendicular to a third line in a plane will intersect at two points.

2. The sum of the angles of a triangle is greater than 180°.

3. Two lines intersect at two points.

4. A line has finite length.

The geometry described in the student activity is one discovered by G. F. B. Riemann (1826–1866) 30 years after Bolyai and Lobachevsky independently discovered hyperbolic geometry. These and other geometries are called non-Euclidean geometry to distinguish them from the geometry of the Greeks, named after Euclid, the third-century B.C. mathematician who compiled all the known geometry of his day.

Before Bolyai began to study geometry, he tried a career in the military. On one occasion, he was challenged to a duel by the entire officer contingent of a regiment. Bolyai accepted the duel with the condition that he could play the violin between each individual duel. Whether the music calmed him or unnerved his opponents is unclear, but Bolyai won every duel. Soon after, he was decommissioned, no doubt to spare other officers the same fate.

Extension

Have students compare the shortest direct route between Los Angeles and London on a two-dimensional map to the shortest direct route on a globe. Drawing a line on the map and a line on the globe to directly connect these cities will reveal different routes. As in spherical geometry, the shortest distance between two points on the earth's surface is not a straight line, as it is on a two-dimensional map, but a curved line. Because the curvature of the earth is a factor in long trips, the navigator of an airplane or a ship on a transatlantic trip, for example, will pilot a route along a great circle. A great circle is a circle on the surface of the earth with the same center as the earth. Have students plot the great-circle route between Los Angles and London on the globe, and compare that route with the straight-line route on the two-dimensional map.

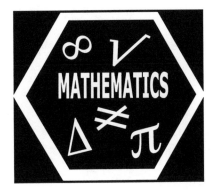

Can It Be True?

Imagine being famous for something you thought was true but couldn't prove. You might wonder how this could possibly happen, but happen it did, to Christian Goldbach (1690–1764), a Russian mathematician born in the town of Konigsberg. His claim to fame is called Goldbach's Conjecture. In mathematics, a conjecture is a statement about a particular mathematical relationship. Though the conjecture may be supported by particular facts, the conjecture itself does not become a fact until the relationship is proven true in every possible case.

Goldbach first revealed his conjecture in a letter to the most famous mathematician of that day, Leonhard Euler (1707–1783). In his letter, Goldbach wrote that he had discovered that any even integer greater than 2 is the sum of two prime numbers. For example, $12 = 7 + 5$. Goldbach had checked his conjecture with hundreds of numbers, for which it was always true, but he couldn't prove that it would be true in every possible case. He asked Euler for help, but Euler couldn't prove it either. To this day, no one has been able to prove that Goldbach's Conjecture is true for every even integer greater than 2. However, no one has found an even integer for which Goldbach's Conjecture is not true. It remains one of the great unsolved problems of mathematics, yet is so easy to state that anyone can understand it.

For this activity, select three even integers between 100 and 200 and show that Goldbach's Conjecture is true for each of them.

Can It Be True?
Teacher Page

Goldbach's Conjecture is one of several unsolved mathematics problems that have haunted mathematicians for centuries. That such a simple mathematical relationship should be so stubborn to prove seems contradictory. Although Goldbach was an accomplished mathematician who regularly corresponded with Euler and made contributions to the theory of curves and integration of differential equations, it is the conjecture for which he is known today. Had he not revealed his conjecture to Euler in that letter, he would simply be a footnote in the history of mathematics. Interestingly, it was in a letter to Goldbach that Euler first showed his famous equation:

$$e^{i\pi} + 1 = 0$$

Another simple mathematical relationship that frustrated mathematicians for centuries was known as Fermat's Last Theorem. The theorem was named for Pierre de Fermat (1601–1665), who wrote the following in the margin of Greek mathematician Diophantus's writings on quadratic equations:

> To divide a cube into two cubes, a fourth power, or in general any power whatever above the second into two powers of the same denomination is impossible, and I have assuredly found an admirable proof of this, but the margin is too narrow to hold it.

One wonders how narrow the margin could have been to allow Fermat to write all that. Regardless, Fermat did not include a proof with his comments. For nearly 350 years, no one could prove his statement. The frustration of countless mathematicians who wished Fermat had had a wider margin was finally answered in 1996, when British mathematician Andrew Wiles proved Fermat's Last Theorem. Wiles used highly complex mathematics to prove it. In the words of colleague Kenneth Ribet, Wiles's process was to "use Hilbert irreducibility and the Cebotarev Density Theorem to produce a non-cuspidal rational point of X over which the covering remains irreducible."

Extension

Before sharing Fermat's Last Theorem with your students, present to them the following list of equations. Ask students to find integer values for the variables in each of the equations. Students will quickly find values for the first two equations, but not for the last three, as Fermat had concluded. Have students write a conjecture based on their findings, and then present Fermat's Last Theorem to the class for comparison.

1. $x^1 + y^1 = z^1$
2. $x^2 + y^2 = z^2$
3. $x^3 + y^3 = z^3$
4. $x^4 + y^4 = z^4$
5. $x^5 + y^5 = z^5$

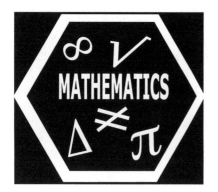

Head in the Clouds

He was walking along, studying the stars. Thales of Miletus (c.624–c.547 B.C.) had already helped the Phoenicians improve their navigation at sea. He told them to focus on the Little Dipper constellation as a navigational aid. He had also predicted the solar eclipse of May 28, 585 B.C. Now he was searching the heavens for more discoveries. Suddenly, the stars disappeared and all went black! Thales, one of the Seven Wise Men of Antiquity, had stepped into a well. Fortunately, he was not injured. Only his pride was hurt.

Thales, the first known mathematician, not only discovered relationships in mathematics, but he proved what he discovered. He showed that the relationships were true in every possible case. Thales made the following five discoveries:

1. A circle is bisected by any diameter.

2. The base angles of an isosceles triangle are equal.

3. Vertical angles are equal.

4. Two triangles are congruent if they have two angles and one included side equal.

5. An angle inscribed in a semicircle is a right angle.

Thales was the first mathematician to study the theoretical basis of mathematics. All mathematicians before him had studied mathematics only in practical applications. Though Thales was a remarkable intellect, he was equally at home in the real world. In fact, the practical wisdom he showed as a young man enabled him to retire at an early age. Once Thales retired, he traveled to Egypt and amazed the local priests with his ability to use geometry to calculate the height of the pyramids. What did he do that brought him early retirement?

One spring, young Thales noticed that all the olive trees in his local district were full of blossoms, ensuring a large olive crop. Speculators quickly bought all the olive groves to take advantage of the coming crop. Thales devised a different plan. Because olive oil was such a staple in the Greek diet, he reasoned that olive oil, not the olives themselves, would generate the most money. So, Thales bought or rented all the olive presses he could find. When the olive crop was harvested, Thales controlled all the presses and made his fortune processing olive oil.

Thales designed a method for determining the distance from the shore to a ship at sea. The diagram below presents an example of how to use Thales's method. For this activity, use similar triangles and the data in the diagram to determine the distance from the shore to the ship.

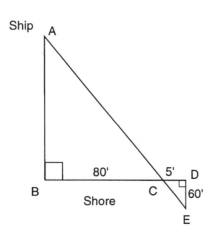

Head in the Clouds
Teacher Page

For the student activity, triangle $ABC \sim$ triangle EDC (they must be similar because they have all three angles in common). Thus, the distance from the shore to the ship, x, is found as follows:

$$\frac{AB}{ED} = \frac{BC}{DC}; \qquad\qquad \frac{x}{60} = \frac{80}{5}; \qquad\qquad x = 960 \text{ feet}$$

Little is truly known about Thales's life except for a few stories and some attributed discoveries. Even the years of his birth and death are open to conjecture. Because none of Thales's writings exist today, it is impossible to be certain about exactly what he wrote and what discoveries he made. However, mathematics historians agree that Thales attempted to generalize his discoveries by proving that they were true in all cases. He is the first known mathematician to establish mathematical relationships through deductive reasoning.

Thales also demonstrated his practical intelligence when he helped a farmer with a stubborn mule. The farmer was going to the market with his mule and a heavy load of salt. While crossing a stream, the mule stumbled and fell into the water. Some of the salt dissolved; when the mule stood up, its load was lighter. At the next stream, the mule stumbled again, and the load became lighter still. By the time the farmer and the mule arrived at the market, the mule had no load at all. After that, every time the mule carried a load, it stumbled into each stream it crossed. The farmer asked Thales for help. Thales's suggestion was to load the mule with sponges. He assured the farmer that, with a load of sponges, one slip into a stream would end the clever mule's stumbling routine!

Extension

The description of how Thales determined the distance from the shore to a ship at sea is ambiguously recorded. Some mathematics historians argue for the following situation instead of the one shown in the student activity:

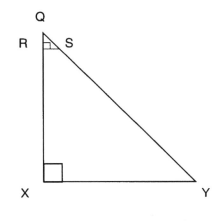

In this diagram, a person (QR) is standing at the top of a tower (RX) looking down at the end (S) of a crosspiece of wood (RS) at a ship (Y) offshore. The two triangles formed by this diagram are similar triangles. Knowing the height of the tower (RX), the height of the person (QR), and the length of the crosspiece (RS), the distance from the shore to the ship (XY) can be calculated using the following proportion:

$$\frac{QR}{QX} = \frac{RS}{XY}$$

Head in the Clouds Teacher Page continues on page 86.

Present the following table to your students without the solutions in the second column. Have them assume that the person viewing down the crosspiece is 6 feet tall and the tower is 54 feet tall. Based on this data, they can determine the distance from shore to a ship according to how long a crosspiece is needed to sight the ship.

Length of Crosspiece (ft.)	Distance from shore to ship (ft.)
3	30
4	40
5	50
7	70

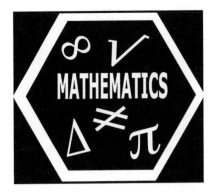

Measuring the Earth

You may have learned that when Christopher Columbus made his great discovery, most people thought he would sail off the edge of the earth. Although some uneducated peasants probably believed that the earth was flat, anyone with at least some education knew the earth was round. They also knew the size of the earth, thanks to the ancient Greek mathematician Eratosthenes (c.276–195 B.C.). In his book *On the Measurement of the Earth* Eratosthenes even showed how he calculated the size of the earth.

Eratosthenes was one of several Greek mathematicians who spent time in Alexandria, Egypt. While there, Eratosthenes heard about a deep well in the town of Syene, located south of Alexandria. On the longest day of the year, the reflection of the sun could be seen at the bottom of the well. On the same day, the sunlight made an angle of 7°12' in Alexandria. Eratosthenes knew that Syene was 5,000 stadia directly south of Alexandria (1 Egyptian stadia, or stadium, is equal to 516.73 feet). Eratosthenes used this information and his knowledge of geometry to calculate the circumference of the earth to within a few hundred miles.

The following diagram illustrates how Eratosthenes found the earth's circumference:

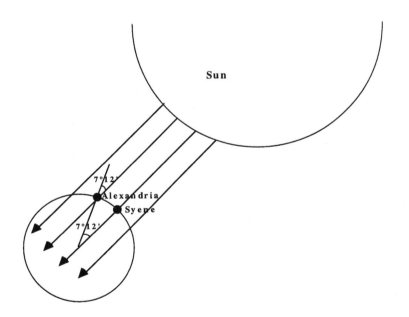

For this activity, use the diagram and Eratosthenes' data to determine the earth's circumference in miles.

Measuring the Earth
Teacher Page

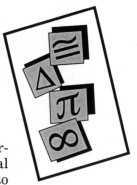

Eratosthenes used the fact that the sun's rays are parallel to determine that the angle of the sun at Alexandria was equal to the central angle shown in the diagram. He then used the following proportion to compute the circumference of the earth:

$$\frac{7\frac{1}{12}{}^\circ}{360^\circ} = \frac{5,000 \; stadia}{x \; stadia}$$

$$\frac{1}{50} = \frac{5,000}{x}$$

$$x = 250,000 \; stadia$$

$$x = 24,466 \; miles$$

Converting 250,000 stadia to miles yields a circumference of 24,466 miles, a measurement close to the actual circumference of the earth: 24,907 miles. Eratosthenes' result was based on slightly erroneous data. Syene is not directly south of Alexandria but actually 3° west of it, and is 4,530 stadia from Alexandria, not 5,000 stadia. Thus, Eratosthenes' method cannot be used with Syene and Alexandria because Syene is not directly south of Alexandria. Regardless, Eratosthenes method is correct, and the circumference he computed is remarkably accurate.

By the time of Columbus, Eratosthenes' results were known by all of educated Europe. Consequently, Columbus found no supporters in any of the courts of Europe until he convinced Queen Isabella of Spain to fund his venture. Even Isabella's advisors counseled against financing Columbus's voyage. Their reason was that the earth was too large to permit sailing to China by a Western route. Columbus's crew would exhaust their provisions long before reaching China. In fact, Columbus made landfall at San Salvadore with only a few days' supply of food and water remaining. Had he not made landfall when he did, he would have been forced to return to Spain.

Extension

Archimedes (287–212 B.C.) was a contemporary of Eratosthenes, and they engaged in a lively correspondence about mathematics. One of Archimedes' discoveries was the mathematics of the lever. He once said, "Give me a place to stand and I will move the earth." By this, he meant that he could determine how long a lever he would need to lift the earth. The components of the lever are illustrated in the following diagram:

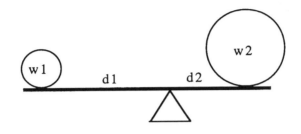

The relationship between weights and distances from the fulcrum of a lever may be expressed as:

$$w_1 \times d_1 = w_2 \times d_2$$

Ask students to determine the length of a lever they would need to lift a 20-ton (40,000-pound) dinosaur. Have them use their own weight as the lifting weight, or lifting force, and assume that the distance from the fulcrum to the dinosaur is 10 feet:

$$40,000 \times 10 = \text{(student weight)} \times \text{(distance from fulcrum to student)}$$

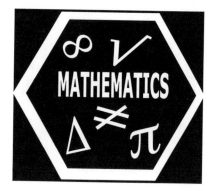

Mathematical Giants

He invented the telescope. He was the best known scientist in all of Italy. His writings about the solar system were circulating throughout Europe. Yet in 1633, he was placed under house arrest by the Catholic Church, confined to his house 24 hours a day. He remained under house arrest for the last nine years of his life. What did Galileo Galilei (1564–1642) do to deserve such confinement? He taught that the sun was at the center of the solar system. Because the Church taught that the earth was at the center of the solar system, and that the sun orbited the earth, Galileo was accused of being a heretic. It was Galileo's misfortune to live in Italy during that time, where the Church still controlled all book printing. Scientists in other countries, such as England and the Netherlands, were able to print Galileo's books without any action by religious or government authorities.

At his trial, Galileo was found guilty of heresy. He pleaded for forgiveness and signed a statement that he was wrong about his claim that the sun was at the center of the solar system. According to legend, when he rose from his knees after signing the statement and begging the Church Court for mercy, Galileo muttered, under his breath, "Nevertheless, the earth does move!"

Galileo is known for his scientific approach to everything he did. He looked for evidence to support or refute any scientific theories of the day. He was the first person to look for evidence to support a theory. For example, for centuries, people had believed that a heavier object would fall faster than a lighter object. Why? Because Aristotle, an ancient Greek philosopher and scientist, had said so. Galileo wasn't so certain. To test this assumption, he climbed to the top of the Leaning Tower of Pisa and dropped two objects of different weights. Just as he had suspected, the objects hit the ground at the same time. They had fallen at the same rate.

Galileo used his scientific approach to determine if giants like King Kong, Godzilla, or Paul Bunyan could exist. He wrote, "If one wants to maintain in a great giant the same proportion of limb as found in an ordinary man, he must find harder or stronger material for making the bones." What did Galileo mean by this statement?

For this activity, build several cubes with blocks. Compare the lengths of their sides and their volumes in the data table below.

Edge length	Volume
1 inch	
2 inches	
3 inches	
4 inches	

Clearly, an increase in weight must come with an increase in volume. Based on the mathematical pattern you found between increase in edge length and increase in volume, compare the increase in volume or weight of a 60-foot-tall human being to a 6-foot-tall human being. Explain why a 60-foot-tall human being couldn't survive.

Mathematical Giants
Teacher Page

Galileo found that human bones are able to support about six times the normal human weight. As we increase in height, our volume (and thus, weight) increases as a cube of the height increase. For the cubes, in the student activity, the volume is found by cubing the edge length of a cube.

A human who is 60 feet tall is 10 times the height of a 6-foot-tall human and so would weigh $10^3 = 1,000$ times as much. This increase in weight and volume is far larger than could be supported by human bones; thus Galileo's comment about needing to have bones made of stronger material if a giant were to exist.

Galileo is best known for his invention of the telescope. Actually, he probably grasped the fundamentals of the telescope when Dutch toy telescopes reached his home city of Venice. Galileo immediately realized the potential for such a device and quickly designed an improved version that was no longer a toy, but a scientific instrument. He also realized the financial value of such a device: Galileo used the telescope to determine the origin of ships sailing for port in Venice while they were still far out on the horizon. Armed with such information, Galileo knew what goods were coming to port and what goods would be bought by arriving ships. This information proved invaluable in a commercial trading city such as Venice, and Galileo took great advantage of it to make wise investments. Soon, however, every merchant in Venice had a telescope, and Galileo's advantage was forever lost.

Extension

Galileo is noted for his applied mathematics rather than any theoretical discoveries. However, his studies also included infinite sets. The concept of infinite sets was a difficult concept for many early mathematicians to fully comprehend. It can still be a counterintuitive concept for many students. For example, most students would suggest that the set of all natural numbers must be twice as large as the set of even natural numbers. To help students understand that both sets are, in fact, infinite sets, and therefore equivalent, ask them to complete the following table. Have students use the data in the completed table to explain how the set of all natural numbers and the set of even natural numbers can be considered equivalent.

All natural numbers: 1 2 3 4 5 20 50 100 500 1,000 10,000

Even natural numbers: 2 4 6 8 10 ? ? ? ? ? ?

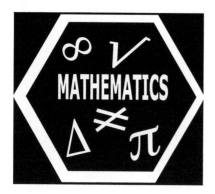

Mathematics to Pass the Time

Being a clerk at the Pennsylvania General Assembly wasn't the most interesting job in the world. In fact, there were times when it was downright boring, especially for a young man who was interested in seeing the wide world around him. Sometimes, things were so dull that he had trouble staying awake. Fortunately, he had something to keep him busy—magic squares. Maybe it was the time spent with magic squares that sharpened his mind. What a mind it was!

Have you ever seen a magic square? They've been around for a long time. According to legend, Emperor Yu of China was the first person to see a magic square, more than 2,000 years ago. Yu was walking along the banks of the Lo River when he saw a large turtle. On the turtle's shell was a magic square. It is impossible to know if any part of this legend is fact. However, the first magic square ever written down appeared in the *Book of Permutations* in China about 400 B.C. Since then, magic squares have been a popular form of recreational mathematics.

The great American patriot Ben Franklin (1706–1790) was the clerk at the Pennsylvania General Assembly who amused himself with magic squares. Franklin wrote that he used them "to avoid weariness." As he grew older, Franklin continued to construct magic squares. In a letter to Peter Collins, Franklin wrote, "I had amused myself in making these kinds of magic squares, and at length had acquired such a knack at it, that I could fill the cells of any magic square, of reasonable size, with a series of numbers as fast as I could write them."

A magic square is a series of integers arranged in a grid so that the sum of the integers in each row, in each column, and in each diagonal totals the same amount. For this activity, complete the empty grid below to make a magic square. Arrange each of the integers from 1 to 9 so that the sum of the numbers in each row, in each column, and in each diagonal totals the same amount. (Hint: First determine the sum of the numbers in each row and column.)

When you find an arrangement of numbers for your magic square, try multiplying each cell in the grid by the same integer. Is the result still a magic square? Try adding the same number to each cell. Is this result still a magic square?

Mathematics to Pass the Time Teacher Page

There is only a single solution to the 3 × 3 magic square from the student activity. Although students will find several seemingly different solutions, all of their solutions will be rotations or reflections of this solution.

8	1	6
3	5	7
4	9	2

If each cell is increased by the same amount or by the same factor, the result is still a magic square.

Although Franklin devoted considerable time and effort to politics, diplomacy, writing, and science, he devoted little time to mathematics. Apparently, the only area of mathematics he explored was magic squares. He was especially proud of the 8 × 8 magic square shown below. However, it is not a true magic square because only the column and row totals are equal (260); the diagonal totals are not. Nevertheless, Franklin's expertise at constructing magic squares earned him an academic honor from the University of Rouen in France. It was Bernard Frenicle de Bessey (1602–1675) who wrote out all 880 magic squares.

52	61	4	13	20	29	36	45
14	3	62	51	46	35	30	19
53	60	5	12	21	28	37	44
11	6	59	54	43	38	27	22
55	58	7	10	23	26	39	42
9	8	57	56	41	40	25	24
50	63	2	15	18	31	34	47
16	1	64	49	48	33	32	17

Extension

A 4 × 4 magic square offers a greater challenge to students, but also offers 880 individual solutions. One well-known 4 × 4 magic square was created by German painter Albrecht Dürer for his painting *Melancholia*. In this magic square, Dürer displayed the date he painted *Melancholia*—1514:

16	3	2	13
5	10	11	8
9	6	7	12
4	15	14	1

Present to students a 4 × 4 magic square showing only the numbers 15 and 14, and ask them to complete the square with the other integers from 1 to 16. Besides the magic square Dürer created, there are at least two others (see below) that show the number 1514. Note how these two magic squares are similar to Dürer's magic square: In the first, two rows have been interchanged; in the second, two columns have been interchanged.

4	15	14	1
5	10	11	8
9	6	7	12
16	3	2	13

13	3	2	16
8	10	11	5
12	6	7	9
1	15	14	4

Mathematics to Pass the Time Teacher Page continues on page 94.

Below is a 14 × 14 magic square.

7	184	19	175	126	114	89	106	66	134	141	148	36	34
190	11	176	22	120	78	88	91	131	57	51	43	159	162
6	188	177	23	76	115	108	105	132	62	50	149	155	33
196	9	15	174	121	79	99	92	65	135	146	48	37	163
5	187	178	75	24	116	98	104	133	61	52	150	161	35
192	12	21	122	173	80	87	93	69	136	145	47	38	164
193	10	18	172	123	81	86	97	68	137	144	46	39	165
4	186	179	25	74	117	110	100	130	60	53	151	158	32
3	185	180	26	157	118	109	103	129	54	59	152	73	31
194	8	17	171	40	82	90	94	67	143	138	45	124	166
2	189	181	27	72	119	107	102	128	58	55	153	156	30
195	13	16	170	125	83	85	95	64	139	142	44	41	167
1	183	182	28	71	113	111	101	127	63	56	154	160	29
191	14	20	169	77	84	112	96	70	140	147	49	42	168

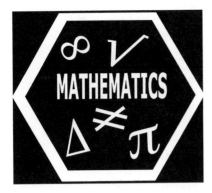

Playing It Safe

If you had a chance to become famous and wealthy, would you take it? What if you had to give up a secure future to take the chance? That's the choice Gilles Personne de Roberval (1602–1675) had. What would you have done? What do you think Roberval did?

Roberval grew up in France. He left home at age 14 and traveled around the country, studying at various universities and tutoring to support himself. Eventually, he moved to Paris and taught at the Collège Royale. Roberval was a talented mathematician who discovered what is now called Cavalieri's Principle. He discovered this principle years before Bonaventura Cavalieri (1598–1647) published his discovery of it. Roberval also determined the area under a curve called a cycloid many years before this discovery was revealed by another mathematician, Evangelista Torricelli. It also seems likely that Roberval had developed a simple approach to calculus long before Newton and Leibnitz published their calculus discoveries. If he made all these discoveries, why isn't Roberval more well known?

The reason concerns a choice Roberval made while he was the Ramus Professor of Mathematics at the Collège Royale. This job was not a secure position. Every three years, a competition was held to determine who should have the position. Thus, every three years, Roberval had to prove that he was still the most worthy applicant for the job. To ensure that he would maintain his professorship, Roberval published none of his discoveries. Instead, he submitted to his competitors mathematics problems that required the knowledge of Roberval's discoveries to solve them. It was a successful tactic: Roberval held his post until his death. One wonders, though, whether Roberval didn't give up potential fame and fortune for the security of his job. What would you have done had you been in Roberval's position?

The diagram below shows a cycloid:

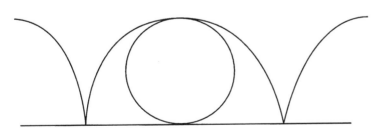

It is formed by tracing the path of a point on the circumference of a circle as the circle rolls along a line. How does the area of the circle compare to the area under one arch of the cycloid? Roberval discovered this relationship in 1634.

For this activity, cut out a cardboard circle, mark a point on the circumference, and then use the circle to trace a cycloid on the same cardboard material. Cut out one arch of the cycloid. If you compare the weights of the circle and the cycloid arch, you will find a ratio that closely approximates the ratio Roberval found. What is it?

Playing It Safe
Teacher Page

Roberval used what he called infinitesimals to determine that the area under one arch of a cycloid is three times the area of the circle that generates it. This result was also found by Galileo (1564–1642), who named the cycloid curve in 1599. Galileo used a method similar to the method students used in the activity. He made a cycloid curve and its generating circle out of wood, and then compared their weights. However, Galileo eventually concluded that the ratio of the two areas was an irrational value close to the integer value 3, but not exactly 3. Roberval computed the ratio and determined that the area under one arch of a cycloid is exactly equal to three times the area of its generating circle.

Galileo's method for finding the area of the cycloid epitomizes his approach to mathematics and science. Galileo was not a great pure mathematician, but a great applied mathematician. In a more modern age, Galileo might have been called an outstanding physicist. For example, one occasion found Galileo atop of the Leaning Tower of Pisa, dropping two objects of different weights. Aristotle had stated that heavier objects fall faster than lighter objects because of their greater weight. Since the time of Aristotle, no one had tried to determine experimentally whether his theory was correct. It was not until Galileo tested Aristotle's statement that anything approaching the modern scientific method was used to verify what were considered scientific facts. Aristotle had theorized incorrectly. Galileo found that all objects fall at the same rate, regardless of weight (see "Mathematical Giants," p. 90).

Extension

Have students test whether objects of different weights fall at the same or different rates by replicating Galileo's famous experiment, perhaps by dropping weights from an upper-story window.

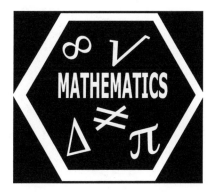

The Puzzle King

He was never known as a mathematician at any time during his life, and the jobs he held were hardly related to mathematics. He was a plumbing contractor and a newspaper columnist. He managed a chain of music stores. He was even a magician and ventriloquist—a friend of circus showman P. T. Barnum. How did Sam Loyd (1841–1911) ever earn the title Puzzle King?

It all began when Loyd was 14. He began to play chess regularly and found that he had a remarkable talent for the game. Within two years, he was regularly contributing chessboard problems to the magazine *Chess Monthly.* From chessboard to problems to mathematics puzzles was a short trip for Loyd. Soon, his puzzles were known across the entire United States. Although he never became wealthy from his puzzles, Sam Loyd became as well known as any entertainer of his day, all thanks to his clever, amusing mathematics puzzles.

A few of Sam Loyd's puzzle problems are presented below. For this activity, solve any two of them and explain your solutions.

1. A lady gives a postage-stamp clerk a $1 bill and says, "Give me some 2¢ stamps, 10 times as many 1¢ stamps, and the balance in 5¢ stamps." How can the clerk fulfill this puzzling request?

2. A bookworm begins eating at page 1 of volume 1 of a 10-volume set of books arranged in order on a bookshelf. The bookworm eats through to the last page of volume 10. Each volume contains 100 pages. Through how many pages did the bookworm eat?

3. A balloon is attached to a wire .01 inch thick. Assume the wire was originally wound in a ball 2 feet in diameter, and further that the wire was wound so solidly that there was no airspace in the ball. Can any of our puzzlists tell us the total length of wire?

4. Fill in all the missing numbers of this division problem:

```
            853
      **9 ) 6*8897
            ***2
            *9**
            **4*
            **4*
            ****
```

The Puzzle King
Teacher Page

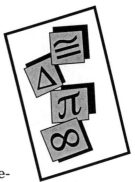

The solutions to the students activity are as follows:

1. The woman has requested at least one 5¢ stamp. Because she wishes to purchase exactly $1 of stamps and at least one 5¢ stamp, the number of 2¢ stamps must be such that the value of these stamps is either a multiple of 5 or 10. For 2¢ stamps, the value must be a multiple of 10, which means that the number of 2¢ stamps must be a multiple of 5. For the number of 2¢ stamps, 10, 15, or more are too many for the problem. Thus, there must be five 2¢ stamps. Given this, the solution is five 2¢ stamps, fifty 1¢ stamps, and eight 5¢ stamps.

2. When the volumes are arranged in order on a shelf, the first page of volume 1 is adjacent to volume 2, and the last page of volume 10 is adjacent to volume 9. The bookworm ate through 800 pages.

3. The unwound wire is actually a cylinder. Thus, the volume of the ball of wire must be equal to the volume of the cylinder of wire:

   Volume of sphere: $\frac{4}{3}\pi r^3$ Volume of cylinder: $\pi r^2 h$

   In inches: $\frac{4}{3}\pi (12")^3 = \pi(0.005")^2 h$

   $h = 92,160,000$ inches (1,454.54 miles)

4.
$$
\begin{array}{r}
853 \\
749\overline{)638897} \\
5992 \\
\hline
3969 \\
3745 \\
\hline
2247 \\
2247 \\
\end{array}
$$

Sam Loyd was not only America's premier puzzlist, but he also invented games. He invented the game Parcheesi and the 14-15 Puzzle. The 14-15 Puzzle consists of 15 tiles numbered from 1 to 15 and contained in a 4-by-4-tile square frame, whereby the space for the "missing" 16th tile allows rearrangement. The tiles must be rearranged so that they appear in consecutive order.

Extension

Sam Loyd had a British counterpart, Henry Ernest Dudeney (1857–1930). Like Loyd, he began his puzzle career with chess problems. Dudeney married in 1884, and his wife became a successful novelist. As a result, Dudeney never had to work to support his family. Freed from the demands of daily employment, Dudeney devoted himself to his mathematics puzzles.

In 1893, he began to correspond with Loyd. For nearly two decades, they engaged in a friendly competition to produce the most interesting mathematics puzzles. Dudeney was a regular puzzle contributor to the magazine *The Strand* for more than 30 years.

Ask your students to solve the following puzzle, one of Dudeney's most famous, which first appeared in 1903:

> In a 30-by-12-by-12-foot rectangular room, a spider is at the middle of one 12-by-12-foot end wall, 1 foot from the ceiling. A fly is at the opposite end wall, 1 foot above the floor. The fly is so frightened it can't move. What is the shortest distance the spider must crawl to capture the fly? (Hint #1: It is less than 42 feet.)
>
> (Hint #2: Make a net of the unfolded room, as shown below.)

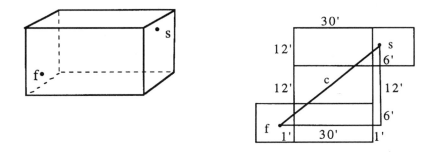

The net of the unfolded room shows that the spider and the fly are at vertices of a right triangle. By the Pythagorean Theorem, $24^2 + 32^2 = c^2$. The shortest distance, c, is 40 feet.

The Unknown Mathematicians

Although mathematics historians can trace present-day mathematics back many centuries, eventually the historical record becomes silent. For example, ancient Egyptian mathematicians made many marvelous discoveries in mathematics, which they used when building their huge statues and, of course, the great pyramids. Yet today, no one knows the name of even one Egyptian mathematician.

What we do know about the mathematics in Egypt comes in the form of a roll of papyrus 18 feet long and 13 inches wide. It is called the Rhind Papyrus, named after Henry Rhind, who purchased it in 1858. When he died, the Rhind Papyrus was sent to the British Museum, where it has been displayed since. The Rhind Papyrus contains 83 mathematics problems about a variety of topics. Some problems are simple computations, such as adding fractions and dividing whole numbers. Other problems involve areas, volumes, and finances, all topics that had everyday applications in ancient Egypt.

The Rhind Papyrus was copied by a scribe named A'hmose. Nothing about him is known, not even the year he copied the papyrus. The best estimate is that he copied it about 1650 B.C. A'hmose wrote that the problems he copied were 200 years old. Thus, they date from at least 1850 B.C., more than 38 centuries ago. The Rhind Papyrus was probably used as a sort of textbook to help an Egyptian student learn common mathematics. Some problems helped the student improve basic computation skills; other problems applied these skills to farming, building construction, and economics.

Four problems from the Rhind Papyrus are presented below. For this activity, solve any three of them.

1. A quantity and its 1/5 added together become 21. What is the quantity?

2. A quantity, its 1/2, and its 1/4 added together become 10. What is the quantity?

3. How many cattle are there in a herd when 2/3 of 1/3 of them make 70, the number due as tribute to the owner? (This is an example of "reckoning" the cattle of a herd.)

4. Sum the geometrical progression of five terms, of which the first term is 7 and the multiplier is 7.

The Unknown Mathematicians
Teacher Page

The solutions to the problems in the student activity are:

1. $17\frac{1}{2}$
2. $5\frac{5}{7}$
3. 315
4. 19,607

Although none of the problems in the Rhind Papyrus show any complex mathematics, they do demonstrate the mathematics of everyday life, and the algorithms used to find solutions. The ancient Egyptian achievements in mathematics are especially impressive considering their inefficient mathematical notation and lack of fractions.

Extension

Another culture that is revealed by a book of mathematics problems is the culture of seventh-century Armenia. The book, *Problems and Solutions of Vardapet Anania of Shirak*, is a collection of 24 problems compiled by Vardapet Anania. His work concerns daily activities and the history of that time, providing a glimpse of life in the Turkish countryside. Two problems from this book are presented below. Ask students to solve them.

1. During the famous Armenian uprising against the Persians, when Zaurak Kamsarakan killed Saurem, one of the Armenian azats (a government official) sent an envoy to the Persian king to report the baleful news. The envoy covered fifty miles in a day. Fifteen days later when he learned of this, Zaurak sent riders in pursuit to bring the envoy back. The riders covered eighty miles in a day. And so, find how many days it took them to catch the envoy. (25 days)

2. My father told me the following story. During the famous wars between the Armenians and the Persians, Prince Zaurak Kamsarakan performed extraordinarily heroic deeds. Three times in a single month he attacked the Persian troops. The first time he struck down half the Persian army, the second time, pursuing the Persians, he slaughtered one fourth of the soldiers. The third time, he destroyed one eleventh of the Persian army. The Persians who were still alive, numbering two hundred eighty, fled to Nakhichevan. And so, from this remainder, find how many Persian soldiers there were before the massacre. (1,760)

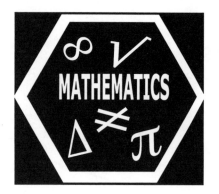

MATHEMATICS

Sleeping In Has Its Benefits

René Descartes (1596–1650), a French mathematician and philosopher, had the perfect schedule—a schedule most people would love to have. He stayed in bed in the morning until he felt ready to get up. Sometimes that wasn't until noon. How would you like to have such a schedule?

Descartes began his late-morning routine when he was a young student at La Fleche, a Jesuit school. When he enrolled there, Descartes's instructors noticed that he was always sick. Yet, if he had the chance to rest in bed for a morning, he seemed to recover his strength. Because Descartes was a superior student and could easily keep up with his classes, the teachers decided to let him sleep in. Descartes kept this schedule into his adult life (see "Too Good to Be True" p. 69).

You might think that Descartes wasted time by spending his mornings in bed, but he didn't. He used the time to think about mathematics and philosophy. In fact, one story about Descartes describes the morning he watched a fly crawl across the ceiling above his bed. Descartes began thinking about how he could describe the location of the fly and the path the fly was taking without making a sketch of the actual path. Eventually, he invented analytical geometry, geometry on coordinate axes, to describe the path of this fly—the most famous fly in the history of mathematics. This new geometry, a milestone in mathematics, combined algebra and traditional geometry into a powerful mathematics tool. Descartes revealed his analytical geometry in his first book, *La Géométrie*, in 1637.

The basic concepts behind Descartes's coordinate geometry are found in many places besides mathematics. For example, the map on page 103 is designed to be used with a grid, or coordinate system, to locate various points of interest in the city of Knoware. For this activity, use the map and grid to find the locations of the following buildings. For example, McDougal's Hamburger Haven is at G3.

1. Dairy Prince Ice Cream

2. Raspberries Record Store

3. Hand Locker Gloves Store

4. M.M. Bean's Clothing

5. Taco Chimes

6. Dippin' Donuts

7. New Army Clothes

	A	B	C	D	E	F	G	H	I	J	K
1											
2				• Dairy Prince Ice Cream							
3							• McDougal's Hamburger Haven				
4	• M.M. Bean's Clothing										
5						• Raspberries Record Store					
6											
7		• Dippin' Donuts									
8											
9							• Hand Locker Gloves Store				
10		• Taco Chimes									
11									• New Army Clothes		

Sleeping In Has Its Benefits
Teacher Page

For the student activity, the coordinates are:

1.   Dairy Prince Ice Cream: D2
2.   Raspberries Record Store: F5
3.   Hand Locker Gloves Store: H9
4.   M.M. Bean's Clothing: A4
5.   Taco Chimes: C10
6.   Dippin' Donuts: B7
7.   New Army Clothes: K11

Descartes actually published his analytical geometry in *Discours de la Methode* in 1637. *La Géométrie*, which contained his discovery, was an addendum to this book. Many individuals who purchased *Discours* found *La Géométrie* difficult to understand and of no practical use. They asked the bindery to remove the entire section from the book. The second printing, in 1638, omitted *La Géométrie* altogether. Despite the difficulties with this section, *Discours* sold quite well. However, Descartes did not become rich from the sales of his book. In fact, he received no royalties from the publisher, having instead agreed to accept as payment 200 free copies of *La Géométrie* to distribute among friends and fellow mathematicians.

Was *La Géométrie* all that difficult to comprehend? Apparently so. In a letter to Marin Mersenne, Descartes wrote about *La Géométrie*: "I have omitted a number of things that might have made it clearer but I did it intentionally, and I would not have it otherwise."

Extension

Descartes's analytical geometry can be used to locate objects in three-dimensional space, with the use of a third axis to show depth. Once two objects have been located in three-dimensional space—represented by two points: (x_1, y_1, z_1) and (x_2, y_2, z_2)—the distance between them can be calculated using the following formula (a modification of the formula for finding distance between two points in two-dimensional space):

$$\text{Distance} = \sqrt{(x_2 - x_1)^2 + (y_2 - y_1)^2 + (z_2 - z_1)^2}$$

Present the formula to your students and have them use it to solve this problem:

> A girl is standing at the center of a bridge as a boat floats directly under her, in a river that is perpendicular to the bridge. The boat is 10 feet below the surface of the bridge. The girl then walks to the end of the bridge. By the time the girl has walked 40 feet from the center of the bridge, the boat has floated 30 feet past the bridge. At this moment, how far is the boat from the girl?

The center of the bridge may be considered the origin of a three-dimensional coordinate system, or (0,0,0). For the problem, when the girl is at (40,0,0), the boat is at (0,–10,30).

$$\text{Distance} = \sqrt{(x_2 - x_1)^2 + (y_2 - y_1)^2 + (z_2 - z_1)^2}$$

$$\text{Distance} = \sqrt{(40 - 0)^2 + (0 - 10)^2 + (0 - 30)^2}$$

$$\text{Distance} = \sqrt{(40)^2 + (-10)^2 + (-30)^2}$$

$$\text{Distance} = \sqrt{1,600 + 100 + 900}$$

$$\text{Distance} = \sqrt{2,600}$$

$$\text{Distance} = 51.0 \text{ feet}$$

Mathematical Rhymes

Imagine a mathematics class without a textbook, a class for which you had to memorize all your mathematics. It seems far-fetched, but this is how mathematics was learned in the India of Aryabhata's day (476–550). Why were there no mathematics textbooks? The reason concerns the social system of India, which is divided into castes. In Aryabhata's time, the Brahmans (the Hindu priests of the higher castes) committed their knowledge to memory to prevent the lower castes from attaining it. In many cases, the Brahmans used poetic verses to more easily remember facts and concepts. Aryabhata's most famous work, *Aryabbatiya* (c.490), was written entirely in verse.

Aryabbatiya represents the development of several centuries of Hindu mathematics in India. It contains information about arithmetic, algebra, trigonometry, continued fractions, and quadratic equations, and includes a table of sines. Aryabhata also computed a value for π that was accurate to four decimal places (3.1416). In *Siddharta*, another of Aryabhata's books, he made a number of accurate observations about the heavens. For example, he wrote that the orbits of the planets around the sun were ellipses, that the planets and the moon shine because they reflect light from the sun, and that the visual rotation of the stars is actually due to the rotation of the earth. He explained the mechanics of lunar and solar eclipses and even determined the length of the year (one orbit around the sun) to within a few minutes. All of this was written in 121 stanzas of verse.

One of Aryabhata's discoveries was a formula for finding the sum of the first n triangular numbers. Triangular numbers are numbers that are shaped like equilateral triangles when represented as a series of points. The first four triangular numbers are shown here:

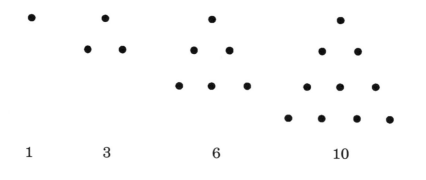

<table>
<tr><td>1</td><td>3</td><td>6</td><td>10</td></tr>
</table>

For this activity, complete the data table below. Use your data to find the formula for the sum of the first n triangular numbers. (Hint: The formula has three factors in the numerator.)

n	Triangular Number	Sum of First n Triangular Numbers
1	1	1
2	3	4
3	6	10
4	10	
5		
6		
7		

Mathematical Rhymes
Teacher Page

The formula for the sum of the first *n* triangular numbers is:

$$\text{Sum} = \frac{n(n + 1)(n + 2)}{6}$$

n	Triangular Number	Sum of First *n* Triangular Numbers
1	1	1
2	3	4
3	6	10
4	10	20
5	15	35
6	21	56
7	28	84

The tradition of writing important facts and concepts in verse continued for several centuries after Aryabhata. The next great Hindu mathematician was Brahmagupta (598–670), and he, too, wrote mathematics and astronomy texts in verse. Whereas Aryabhata wrote a summary of the existing mathematics of his day, Brahmagupta showed a remarkably advanced understanding of mathematics, and wrote about many specific concepts. For example, Brahmagupta was the first mathematician to write about the concept of zero. His best-known work, *Brahma-Sphuta-Siddharta* ("The Opening of the Universe"), contained 21 chapters, each chapter written in verse. In this text, Brahmagupta recorded algorithms for solving quadratic equations and listed rules for adding, subtracting, multiplying, and dividing negative numbers. He included applications of the Pythagorean Theorem, and used algebra to calculate the movements of the planets.

Extension

One of Brahmagupta's best-known discoveries is his formula for finding the area of a cyclic quadrilateral. A cyclic quadrilateral is a quadrilateral for which each vertex lies on the circle. In the figure on page 109, quadrilateral *ABCD* is a cyclic quadrilateral (vertices *A*, *B*, *C*, and *D* lie on circle *O*).

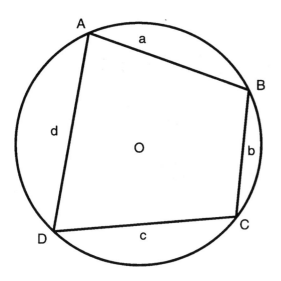

Brahmagupta's formula for finding the area of quadrilateral *ABCD* is:

$$Area = \sqrt{(s-a)(s-b)(s-c)(s-d)}$$

In the formula, a, b, c, and d represent the lengths of the sides of the quadrilateral, and s represents the semiperimeter, or half the perimeter, of the quadrilateral:

$$s = \frac{a+b+c+d}{2}$$

Have students construct a cyclic quadrilateral and measure the lengths of its sides. Have them use Brahmagupta's formula to find the area of the quadrilateral.

The World's Most Expensive Math Lesson

A basic knowledge of mathematics can help you make good decisions. Suppose you had to choose between $3 million or some pennies on a chessboard. Which would you take? Actually, the pennies are arranged on the chessboard in a special way. There is one penny on the first square, two pennies on the second square, four pennies on the third square, eight pennies on the fourth square, and so on. Each square holds twice as many pennies as the previous square. Would you take the pennies or the $3 million?

This problem is similar to the one that the legendary inventor of chess, Grand Vizier Sissa Ben Dahir, gave to his king. When word reached King Sirhan of India that Sissa had invented such a marvelous game, the king wanted to reward him. He asked Sissa what he wanted. Sissa told the king that he wanted some wheat grains on a chessboard, arranged like the pennies in the problem described above. The king asked Sissa whether he didn't want something more, but Sissa insisted on having a chessboard covered with wheat grains. The king reluctantly agreed to grant his wish. The king had hoped to give the inventor of such a brilliant game more than a "handful" of wheat grains.

Sissa chose the wheat instead of gold, jewels, or fame. Was Sissa giving up a chance to be rich? If you were to take the pennies instead of the $3 million, would you be giving up a chance to be rich? Use a calculator to determine how many pennies would lie on square 15. On square 20? Based on your answers, explain whether you would take the pennies or the $3 million. Explain why Sissa Ben Dahir's lesson to the king was the most expensive math lesson in history.

The World's Most Expensive Math Lesson Teacher Page

Students will find that square 15 holds $163.84 and square 20 holds $5,242.88. If some students still think that taking the $3 million is the better choice, have them continue to determine the value of the pennies on each square. Square 30 holds $5,368,709.12. Square 64 holds approximately $92,000,000,000,000,000.00. The filled chessboard holds $184,467,446,737,095,516.15. What about Sissa's request? The filled chessboard holds 18,446,744,673,709,551,615 grains of wheat, enough to cover the entire surface of the earth to a depth of more than two centimeters. Clearly, the king could not grant Sissa's wish. Evidently, Sissa did not really want a reward; he wanted the opportunity to teach his monarch some mathematics. He certainly succeeded.

Extension

Students may have heard how Dutch explorer Peter Minuet "bought" the island of Manhattan in 1624 from a group of Native Americans for some beads and trinkets worth about $24.00. It appears that this was certainly the biggest bargain in history. Yet, suppose the Native Americans could have invested that money at 8% interest, compounded daily. Ask students whether $24.00 would still have been such a great bargain. Would they rather own the entire island of Manhattan and all its buildings or the money from the invested $24.00? Have students determine what the investment would be worth today, using the formula:

$$A = p(1 + \frac{r}{n})^{nt}$$

In this formula, A represents the total value of the investment after t years (for this problem, t is determined by subtracting 1,624 from the present year), p represents the amount invested ($24.00), r represents the percent rate (8%), and n represents the number of times the principal is compounded yearly (365). If the $24.00 had been invested as described, it would be worth more than $235 trillion today, more than enough to buy back the island of Manhattan and all its buildings.

It's All in the Signs

You might not have realized it, but when you write mathematics equations, you are actually writing in a foreign language. This language is understood throughout the world, in every country. The familiar symbols (such as +, ÷, =, and −) are universally recognized. Have you ever wondered how old such symbols are, or who invented them? You may be surprised to learn that most of the symbols we use today are less than 500 years old. How did mathematicians write equations before these symbols were invented? They wrote out their equations using all words. For example, in 1545, Italian mathematician Girolamo Cardano wrote the following equation:

cubus $\overline{\text{p}}$ rebus aequalis 20

Imagine trying to solve this equation using words! In modern notation, the equation looks like this:

$x^3 + 6x = 20$

Shortly after Cardano published the above equation, the equal-sign was invented by English mathematician Robert Recorde (1510–1558), who was also the royal physician to King Edward VI. Recorde's best-known work was *The Whetstone of Witte* (1557), a book full of arithmetic and elementary algebra problems. A whetstone is used to sharpen cutting blades, so the title indicates that the book was meant to sharpen one's wits. Unlike many mathematicians of his day, Recorde wrote it in common English instead of the more scholarly Latin. Because *Whetstone* was written in the common language, it reached a wide audience. In *Whetstone*, Recorde introduced his equal-sign as follows:

> And to avoide the tediouse repetition of these woordes: is equalle to: I will sette as I doe often in work use, a paire of parallels or Gemowe lines of one length, thus: ___ bicause noe 2 thyngs can be moare equalle.

Notice that Recorde introduced the word *Gemowe* to refer to the pair of parallel lines. Ultimately, though, this word never became part of the mathematics vocabulary.

One of the problems from *Whetstone* is presented below. For this activity, assume that an *ob* is equal to a penny, and determine how much to pay for the horse.

> If I sold unto you a horse having 4 shoes and in every shoe 6 nayles, with this condition that you shall pay for the first nayle 1 ob, for the second nayle 2 ob, for the third nayle 4 ob, and so fourth, doubling untill the end of all the nayles, now I ask you, how much would the price of the horse come unto?

It's All in the Signs
Teacher Page

The solution to the student activity is similar to the problem of wheat grains on a chessboard (see "The World's Most Expensive Math Lesson," p. 110). The horse costs $167,772.15.

Although we now use Recorde's symbol for the equal-sign, it was not quickly accepted in Recorde's time. The next mathematician to use it was William Oughtred in 1618. It is because Oughtred also used = for the equal-sign that Recorde's symbol finally became popularly accepted. If Oughtred had used some other symbol for the equal-sign, it is unlikely that Recorde's symbol would be used today. Oughtred invented several of the symbols we use today, among them × for multiplication, :: for a proportion, ∥ for parallel, and ± for plus or minus. Recorde not only wrote in the common vernacular of the people, he was also the first mathematician to describe pen-and-paper algorithms. In *The Grounde of Artes* (1541), Recorde outlined computations using an abacus and also using pen and paper.

Recorde died at a relatively young age while imprisoned in London Tower. The actual events surrounding his death are not certain, but it seems that he encountered some difficulty in his capacity as Surveyor of Mines and Monies for Ireland. Recorde charged the earl of Pembroke, a close friend of the king, with malfeasance. After the earl sued Recorde for libel and won, Recorde was fined £1,000. For failure to pay the fine, he was imprisoned in London Tower, as befitted a man of his scholarly stature. He died shortly after his incarceration. Some historians claim that he died of natural causes, while others are skeptical and suggest that perhaps political intrigue may have contributed to his death.

Extension

Many of the problems in *Whetstone* are cistern problems. They were a popular type of problem in many countries during that time. A typical cistern problem is included here. Ask your students to solve it.

> A cistern has two drain pipes. One pipe can drain the cistern in 5 hours; the other pipe can drain it in only 3 hours. Determine how long it will take both pipes, working together, to drain the cistern.

The drainage rates per hour for the pipes are, respectively, 1/5 and 1/3 of the cistern. The combined drainage rate is 8/15 of the cistern per hour. Thus, solve for x in the following equation:

$$\frac{8}{15}x = 1; \quad x = 1\frac{7}{8} \text{ hours}$$

The Unschooled Mathematician

The year was 1791, and everyone was anxious to begin building the nation's new capital on the banks of the Potomac River. Washington would be the first capital of any nation that had been planned from its very conception. George Washington and Congress had commissioned a team to produce a design for the streets, malls, and parks of the new city. The head of the design team was an expert French architect, Pierre L'Enfant, to ensure that the city was properly designed. L'Enfant was a brilliant but temperamental architect who was always arguing with someone. Just as the surveying was completed, L'Enfant got into another argument, this time with Washington himself. L'Enfant became so angry that he sailed for France, taking all the plans for the nation's capital with him. Starting over was an option, but that would delay the actual building of the capital for many months. Help came from a most unusual source, African American Benjamin Bannekar (1731–1806).

Bannekar was born in Maryland to free African American parents. His mother had been born to freed slaves, and his father had bought his freedom. Bannekar attended elementary school as a young boy, but as soon as he was old enough to work at his parents' farm, he quit school. However, he didn't stop learning. Every day after work, Bannekar read about history, English, or mathematics. He had a natural ability in mathematics and was soon known in his community as the man who could solve any arithmetic problem. When he was 22, Bannekar built a working clock completely from wood, using a pocket watch as a guide for carving all the gears.

When Bannekar was in his 40s, the Ellicott family moved into his county. George Ellicott heard about Bannekar's natural talents and loaned him his mathematics books and astronomical instruments. Soon, Bannekar was gathering his own astronomical data. When George's cousin, Andrew Ellicott, was asked to lead the commission to design Washington, he invited Bannekar to be part of the team. That was a fortunate decision. When L'Enfant left with all the plans, Bannekar simply redrew the plans of the entire city from memory.

Bannekar enjoyed solving problems involving number theory. Two of his problems are presented below. For this activity, solve one of the problems and explain your method for solving it.

1. A hare has a head start equal to the distance a hound covers in 30 leaps. The hare leaps 4 times for 3 leaps by the hound, but every 2 leaps by the hound cover as much ground as the hare can cover in 3 leaps. How many leaps must the hound make to overtake the hare? But wait! Just as the hound reaches the hare, the hare turns. At each turn, the hare gains another 3 hound-leaps head start, and the hare makes 6 turns in all.

2. A gentleman sent his servant with £100 to buy 100 animals, with orders to give £5 for each bullock, 20 shillings for each cow, and one shilling for each sheep. (Recall that 20 shillings = £1.) What number of each sort of animal did he bring back to his master?

The Unschooled Mathematician
Teacher Page

The problems for the student activity are similar to problems that appeared in ancient Egypt and Greece, in Arabic mathematics of the tenth century, and in medieval European texts. The solutions are:

1. 432 hound-leaps

2. 19 bullocks, 1 cow, and 80 sheep

In the history of mathematics, Bannekar is most certainly the mathematician who had the least amount of formal education. He was self-taught to an extent unequaled by any other mathematician. One can only wonder what he might have accomplished with university training. The full extent of his achievements in mathematics will never be known because few of Bannekar's mathematics writings have survived. On the day of his funeral, Bannekar's house caught fire and burned to the ground. The fire destroyed all his notes and manuscripts.

While he was helping to design Washington, Bannekar was also collecting data for an almanac. His first almanac was well received, and he produced yearly almanacs for the next decade. Bannekar sent a copy of his first almanac, *Benjamin Bannekar's Pennsylvania, Delaware, Maryland, and Virginia Almanac for the Year of Our Lord 1792*, to Thomas Jefferson, along with a letter pleading for the rights of the thousands of slaves in the United States. In a letter to Bannekar, Jefferson responded, "Nobody wants more than I do to see such proofs as you exhibit that nature has given to our black brethren talents equal to those of the other colors of men." Jefferson was so impressed with the almanac that he sent it to French mathematician Marie Jean Condorcet of the French Academy of Science in Paris, the most respected group of scientists in the world.

Extension

The problem that follows is another of the type Bannekar liked to solve. His solution method for such problems was lost in the fire that destroyed his house. He might have solved them using trigonometry. Ask students to solve the problem with and without trigonometry.

A 60-foot ladder placed between two walls reaches a 37-foot-high window on one wall. Tilting the ladder to the other wall, without moving the bottom of the ladder, it reaches a 23-foot-high window. How far apart are the walls? (102.65 feet)

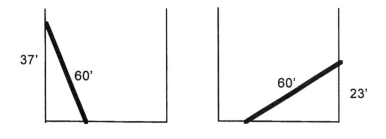

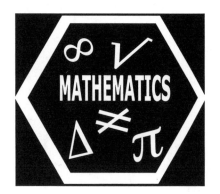

The Most Learned Scholar of His Time

Would you be nervous if you were a teacher and Charlemagne, the future Emperor of the Holy Roman Empire, were one of your students? Maybe not. What if Charlemagne weren't a child, but a fully grown adult who was already the King of France and soon to be Emperor? Now would you be nervous? Probably. Alcuin of York (735–804), though, wasn't the least bit nervous.

Alcuin of York was the most famous scholar in all of Europe. He wrote books about arithmetic, geometry, and astronomy at a time when learning in Europe was just beginning to awaken after centuries of darkness. It was Alcuin, in fact, who led the rebirth of learning throughout Europe.

Alcuin attended the cathedral school in York, England, as a boy and became its headmaster in 778. While he was headmaster, Alcuin transformed the school into the most important center of learning in Europe. In 781, he was invited by King Charlemagne of France to be head of the Palace School in Aachen, France. While Alcuin was in Aachen, Charlemagne was one of his students. In a letter to his most famous pupil, Alcuin wrote to Charlemagne, "I have sent to you, majesty, some figures of arithmetical subtlety for your enjoyment."

What Alcuin included with his letter to Charlemagne has been lost, but he probably sent some problems like the 53 arithmetic puzzles in his book *Propositions for Quickening a Young Mind.* Several of the problems from Alcuin's book are presented below. For this activity, solve any three of them and explain your solutions.

1. A dog is chasing a rabbit which has a start of 150 feet. The dog jumps 9 feet every time the rabbit jumps 7 feet. In how many leaps does the dog overtake the rabbit?

2. If 100 bushels of corn can be distributed among 100 people in such a manner that each man receives 3 bushels, each woman 2, and each child 1/2, how many men, women, and children were there?

3. When a farmer goes plowing and has turned three times at each end of his field, how many furrows has he plowed?

4. An old man met a child, "Good day, my son," he said. "May you live as long again as you have lived, and as long again, and thrice as much as the sum of the last two, and then if God gives you one year more, you will be just a century old." How old was the boy?

The Most Learned Scholar
of His Time
Teacher Page

The solutions to the problems for the student activity are:

1. 75 jumps

2. 11 men, 15 women, and 74 children

3. 7 furrows

4. 11 years old

Alcuin did not discover any original mathematics. In fact, his writings seem designed as introductory material for someone just beginning a study of mathematics. However, considering the then dormant state of learning across Europe, Alcuin deserves to be called the most renowned scholar of his time.

While at the Palace School, Alcuin instituted changes in the educational system throughout Charlemagne's kingdom. He directed that every abbey and monastery had to maintain its own school. He devised the curriculum for these schools to include arithmetic, geometry, astronomy, music, grammar, rhetoric, and logic. Alcuin even wrote the textbooks that were to be used in church schools. One long-lasting result of Alcuin's reforms has been the Carolingian script. Alcuin introduced it to ensure a script that could be easily read and written. The Carolingian script is the source of our modern printed alphabet.

Until he retired to St. Martin's of Tours in 796, Alcuin also taught classes at the Palace School. Some of his students, in addition to Charlemagne, included members of the royal family and sons of the nobility.

Extension

One of Alcuin's problems that Charlemagne may have tried to solve or even acted out with his family members is the following:

> A wolf, a goat, and a cabbage must be transported across a river in a boat holding only one of these things besides the ferryman. How must he carry them across so that the goat shall not eat the cabbage, nor the wolf the goat?

The Most Learned Scholar of His Time Teacher Page continues on page 118.

This problem is similar to a problem written by Nicolo Tartaglia (see "A Difficult Childhood," p. 52). Ask students to solve the problem. Then, assign roles to students and have them act out the solution. Let F represent the ferryman, W the wolf, G the goat, and C the cabbage. For convenience, assume that the river is oriented north to south, and that the merchant must cross from the west bank, the left side of $|$, to the east bank, the right side of $|$.

1. All are on the west bank of the river. $F \, W \, G \, C \mid$

2. The ferryman takes the goat to the east bank. $W \, C \mid F \, G$

3. The ferryman returns to the west bank. $F \, W \, C \mid G$

4. The ferryman takes the cabbage to the east bank. $W \mid F \, G \, C$

5. The ferryman returns to the west bank with the goat. $F \, W \, G \mid C$

6. The ferryman takes the wolf to the east bank. $G \mid F \, W \, C$

7. The ferryman returns to the west bank. $F \, G \mid W \, C$

8. The ferryman takes the goat to the east bank. $\mid F \, W \, G \, C$

A Puzzling Will

Just a few months ago, he and his wife had been overjoyed at expecting their first child. Then he had become ill. It didn't seem he was getting well. In fact, he was becoming sicker. Although he was not an old man, he suspected that he might not live to see the birth of his first child. It was time to make a will. That was crucial. In the Persian city where Islamic mathematician Al-Khwarizimi (c.790–840) lived, a husband's possessions were forfeited to the local ruler unless he had a will. Al-Khwarizimi dictated a will that provided for both his wife and his unborn child. In Persia, the matter of inheritance was important. The more specific the will, the better. Al-Khwarizimi's will was brief and to the point.

You may not have heard of Al-Khwarizimi. He was the first in a series of Islamic mathematicians who kept alive the mathematics and science of the ancient Greeks. They translated the Greek manuscripts into Arabic. Without their translations, all that knowledge would have been lost. They also advanced mathematics and science, especially algebra and astronomy. The Islamic mathematicians even included Chinese and Hindu discoveries in their writings. For example, Al-Khwarizimi wrote about the concept of zero. He probably learned about this concept when he served as a diplomat in India.

What about Al-Khwarizimi's will? He stipulated that if his wife gave birth to a son, 2/3 of his estate was to be given to the son. The remaining 1/3 of his estate would be given to his wife. If his wife gave birth to a girl, 2/3 of his estate would be given to his wife, and the remaining 1/3 to his daughter. All was in order, or so it seemed. Soon after Al-Khwarizimi died, his wife gave birth to twins: a boy and a girl! His will didn't cover this possibility, or did it?

Could you divide Al-Khwarizimi's estate so that his property would be given to his family as he had wished? For this activity, explain how to use the stipulations of Al-Khwarizimi's will to divide the inheritance among his wife, son, and daughter.

A Puzzling Will
Teacher Page

Very specific inheritance laws are part of the Koran. Because of this, the greatest part of Al-Khwarizimi's book, *Hisab Al-Jabr w'Al-Muqabalah,* dealt with the settlement of inheritance disputes. As a result of his experience in these matters, Al-Khwarizimi wrote a very succinct will. Clearly, Al-Khwarizimi wanted a son to inherit twice as much as his wife, and a daughter to inherit half as much as his wife. Thus, if the daughter receives a single share of the estate, x, the wife should receive twice as much as the daughter, or $2x$, and the son should receive twice as much as the wife, or $4x$. If the estate is divided into seven shares in this manner, Al-Khwarizimi's family would receive portions of the estate as he had stipulated. That is, the son receives 4/7 of the estate, the wife 2/7, and the daughter 1/7.

Al-Khwarizimi (actually Abu Jafar Muhammed ibn Musa al-Khwarizimi, meaning "Mohammed, the father of Jafar and the son of Musa, the Khwarizimian") was from the Persian province of Khoresm, just south of the Aral Sea. Al-Khwarizimi is the source of two common mathematics terms, *algebra* and *algorithm*. The term *algebra* is derived from the word *al-jabr* in the title of Al-Khwarizimi's masterwork *Hisab Al-jabr w'Al-Muqabalah*. Loosely, the title means "the setting of equations which have been broken." In other words, it was a book about solving equations. It was in this book that Al-Khwarizimi discussed the Hindu concept of zero. The term *algorithm* is derived from a Latin translation of this book. In this translation, several instances of quoting Al-Khwarizimi began, "Thus has spoken Algoritmi [a transliteration of Al-Khwarizimi's name]."

Al-Khwarizimi was also indirectly responsible for introducing the concept of zero to western Europe. When he was a young man, Al-Khwarizimi served as an ambassador to the city of Khazarin, Empire of Kazars, which was located between the Caspian Sea and the Black Sea on a major trade route to India and China. It may be that Al-Khwarizimi first learned about the concept of zero from Indian diplomats while at his post in this city. In 1126, Adelard of Bath traveled from England to Spain and translated Al-Khwarizimi's masterwork into Latin. His translation introduced Al-Khwarizimi, and the concept of zero, to western European mathematicians.

Extension

Throughout his life, Al-Khwarizimi wrote about mathematics. It was his knowledge of mathematics that was especially useful for his role as court astrologer to Caliph Al-Wathiq. In this position, Al-Khwarizimi gave advice to the caliph about a variety of subjects. A day came when the caliph, seriously ill, sent for Al-Khwarizimi and asked if he would survive his sickness. To Al-Khwarizimi, it appeared as if the caliph was fatally stricken and would not recover. To tell the caliph so might mean Al-Khwarizimi's life because, in the Persia of Al-Khwarizimi's time, the bearer of bad news was frequently treated as if he were the cause of it. Present Al-Khwarizimi's predicament to your students and have them offer a solution.

Not only was Al-Khwarizimi a genius in mathematics, but he also had a practical intelligence, which he used in this case. Al-Khwarizimi told the caliph that he would continue to rule. Relieved, the caliph dismissed Al-Khwarizimi, only to die 10 days later. The caliph's death did not, however, adversely affect Al-Khwarizimi's reputation. Contrarily, because the caliph had indeed continued to rule, even though for only 10 days, Al-Khwarizimi became more revered. He had been correct in his prediction, and he had kept his life with a practical decision.

One Fine Day

Most people happily anticipate particular days, such as a birthday, the beginning of a vacation, or some special event. For the townsfolk of Lochau, Prussia, the date was October 3, 1533. On that day, a large group of men, women, and children gathered on a hilltop at dawn, awaiting the final stage of their eternal destiny. They had rid themselves of all worldly possessions and were expecting a chariot to take them to heaven. How had they come to this decision? The answer concerns German mathematician Michael Stifel (1486–1567).

Stifel graduated from the University of Wittenberg in 1511. He became a monk at the monastery of Esslingen, but soon left to join the Protestant followers of Martin Luther. Stifel became a friend of Luther's and even stayed at Luther's house in Wittenberg for a time. Eventually, Luther installed Stifel as pastor in Lochau in 1528. After a few years, Stifel began to apply his mathematical knowledge to the Bible and Bible prophecy. He calculated the date when the world would end. Early in January 1533, Stifel began to tell the members of his parish to prepare for October 3—the date when those with faith would receive their eternal salvation in heaven, the date when the world would end.

As dawn of October 3, 1533, arrived, the faithful believers of Lochau, and many believers from other towns, met on the hilltop. The air was charged with excitement as they waited for the hour of 8 A.M., the time that they would all be taken to heaven, as calculated by Stifel. These people had sold their homes and worldly possessions in preparation for this day. Some had even burned down their houses so they would not be distracted from their goal of salvation. The day progressed, but no heavenly chariot appeared. Stifel managed to drift away from the crowd and hurry to town, where he convinced the local constable to lock him in jail, where he would be safe from the irate mob that soon followed. Cooler heads prevailed, though, and Stifel was able to leave the safety of his cell. Eventually, Stifel gained Luther's forgiveness and was even installed as pastor in Holzdorf, Germany. He was given strict orders to never again use his mathematics to prophesy.

While living in Holzdorf, Stifel wrote the mathematics text that brought him fame throughout Germany. In 1544, he published *Arithmetica Integra*, the most thorough treatment of algebra to that date. In it, he instituted the practice of arranging powers of an unknown quantity in descending order on one side on an equation set equal to zero (for example: $3x^4 + 2x^3 - 5x^2 + 3x + 3 = 0$). In *Arithmetica*, Stifel anticipated the use of symbols for exponents, and used, for example, $AAAA$ to represent A^4. He did not, however, have a grasp of irrational numbers, writing that "an irrational number is not a true number, but lies hidden in some sort of cloud of infinity." Although Stifel solved quadratic equations with negative roots, he considered such roots as *numeri absurdi*—"absurd numbers."

The problem below is an example of the problems Stifel solved that resulted in negative solutions. For this activity, solve the problem and explain, based on your solution, why Stifel considered negative numbers to be "absurd" numbers.

One side of a rectangular garden is 3 yards longer than the other side. The area of the garden is 270 square yards. What are the dimensions of the garden?

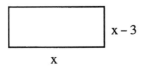

One Fine Day
Teacher Page

The problem for the student activity results in the following equation and solution:

$$\text{Area} = bh \ (\text{base} \times \text{height})$$

$$270 = x \, (x - 3)$$

$$270 = x^2 - 3x$$

$$0 = x^2 - 3x - 270$$

$$0 = (x + 15)(x - 18)$$

$$x = -15, 18$$

A solution of −15 yards for this problem is meaningless because distances must be positive values. As a consequence of such results, and because negative numbers had no real-world applications in Stifel's day (they would not be used in such applications as finance and temperature for many years), Stifel considered all negative numbers to be meaningless, or absurd.

It is difficult to understand why a mathematician such as Stifel would use mathematics to prophesy, but he was not the only mathematician to make such an attempt. One century later, Johannes Kepler applied his mathematics to the Bible to determine the date of the world's demise. Kepler's prediction, though, was perhaps better than Stifel's, because the date of Kepler's prediction was well beyond his lifespan. Thus, unlike Stifel, he did not live to reap the consequences due a false prophet.

Another mathematician who ventured beyond the world of mathematics was French mathematician Michael Chasles (1798–1880), who was a professor at the École Polytechnique and, later, at the prestigious Sorbonne, both in Paris. He wrote about projective geometry, projective transformations, and enumerative geometry. All of Chasles's mathematical expertise, though, did not prevent his being duped by con artist and forger Denis Vrain-Lucas. In the 1860s, Chasles bought more than 27,000 letters, documents, and manuscripts supposedly written by Plato, Alexander the Great, Cleopatra, Judas Iscariot, and Atilla the Hun, among other famous personages. Alas, Chasles's head for figures did not immediately extend to common sense: The fact that all the papers were written in then-modern French did not arouse his suspicions. Only when Vrain-Lucas tried to sell to Chasles documents that he claimed were a series of letters between Blaise Pascal and Sir Isaac Newton did Chasles realize his foolishness. By that time, though, Chasles had already spent 140,000 francs for worthless forgeries.

Extension

Your students might be interested to know how Stifel used his mathematics to prophesy. For example, Stifel linked then Pope Leo X with the number of the Beast in the Bible book Revelations. Beginning with the words *LEO DECIMVS*, the Latin rendering of the name Leo X, Stifel discarded all letters that were not Roman numerals, resulting in *LDCIMV*. From these, he discarded *M*, because it represented the Latin word *mysterium* (meaning "mystery"), and then added *X*, to represent the *X* in the name Leo X, and because *LEO DECIMVS* contains 10 letters. The result was *LDCIVX*.

Ask your students to write these letters in descending magnitude as Roman numerals, and then to add together the Arabic-numeral equivalents. They will obtain the number of the Beast: 666. As an added exercise, have students each use the same procedure to determine the "Stifel number" for their name.

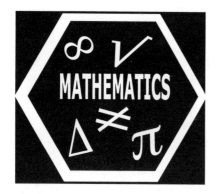

Ahead of His Time

Heron was a Greek mathematician and an inventor. What an inventor he was! He discovered how to use steam to operate a variety of machines. In his book *Pneumatica*, he described more than 100 steam-powered machines, such as a horseless carriage, a robot that served wine, and a wind organ. He invented an automatic door opener and an automatic fireplace lighter. He designed a steam-powered fire engine and even a coin-operated machine that moved figurines about a platform. How long ago do you suppose it was that he invented all these machines? One hundred years ago? Two hundred years ago? Would you believe, nearly 2,000 years ago?

Heron of Alexandria (c.65–c.125) discovered how to harness steam, which he used to power all manner of vehicles and contraptions. Most of his inventions were designed to amuse the ruling class in Alexandria, Egypt. For instance, he developed steam-powered water fountains that shot water high into the air. As you might expect, Heron's mathematics books concerned practical applications of the subject, such as mechanics, engineering, and measurement.

One of Heron's discoveries in mathematics involved minimum paths. A minimum path is the shortest route connecting three or more points. For example, in the diagram below, imagine that points *A* and *B* are two new houses on a new street, represented by line *l*. The telephone company will soon place a telephone pole (point *T*) on the street, and then connect one wire to each of the two houses. Where should the telephone pole (point *T*) be placed so that the total length of the two wires is as short as possible? In other words, where should point *T* be located so that the path from *A* to *T* to *B* is a minimum path?

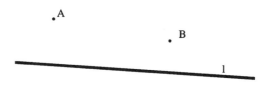

For this activity, find this minimum-path location for point *T* on line *l*. Explain how you determined this location. (Hint: Heron wrote about minimum-path problems in his book *Catoptrica*. Most of this book concerned mirrors and reflections.)

Ahead of His Time
Teacher Page

One solution to the student activity is to reflect point *A* across line *l* to plot point *A'*:

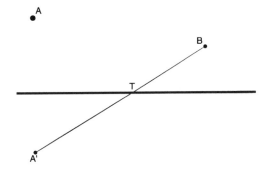

Thus, segment *A'B* represents the minimum distance from *A* to the street (represented by segment *A'T*) and then to point *B*. Point *T* is located by finding the intersection of segment *A'B* and line *l*. If the telephone pole is located at point *T*, the telephone company will use the shortest total length of wire possible.

The same result will be obtained by reflecting point *B* across line *l* to plot point *B'*. Segment *B'A* also intersects line *l* at point *T*:

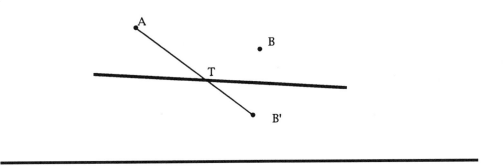

Heron wasn't always practical with his mathematics and inventions. He designed mirrors that reflected images upside down, mirrors that showed the back of the viewer's head, and even mirrors that added an eye or a nose to the viewer's image.

Ahead of His Time Teacher Page continues on page 128.

Extension

Heron's greatest work was *Metrica*. Like so many other works by ancient Greek mathematicians, it became known only from references to it by later mathematicians. However, in 1896, a copy of *Metrica* dating from the eleventh or twelfth century was found in Constantinople. The three books of *Metrica* concern areas of polygons, volumes and surface areas of solids, and the ratios of surface areas to volumes for solids. In *Metrica*, Heron revealed his formula for finding the area of a triangle given the lengths of its three sides:

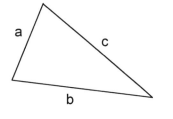

$$\text{Area} = \sqrt{s(s-a)(s-b)(s-c)}$$

In the formula, a, b, and c represent the lengths of the sides of the triangle, and s represents the semiperimeter, or half the perimeter, of the triangle:

$$s = \frac{a+b+c}{2}$$

(To assist in the application of this area formula, Heron even included an algorithm for computing square roots.)

Present to students Heron's formula for finding the area of a triangle. Ask them to find a triangular shape at home, at school, or in their neighborhood; make a sketch of the triangle; and use Heron's formula to determine its area.

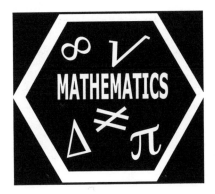

An Apple Makes Mathematics

You have probably heard about the great English mathematician Sir Isaac Newton (1642–1727). Maybe you have also heard that when an apple hit him in the head, he discovered the law of gravity. This apple story sounds like a fairy tale, doesn't it? Most people think so. You might be surprised to know that there is a lot of truth to it.

Newton was a student at Cambridge University when the Plague struck London. To save as many lives as possible, the university was closed and all the students, including Newton, were sent home. During the next two years, in the isolation of his country home in Woolsthorpe, Newton discovered the laws of universal gravitation, invented calculus, and described the nature of light. Never before or since has one person made such significant discoveries, and in such a brief period of time.

What about the apple? Dr. William Stukeley, a friend of Newton's and a physician who belonged to the Royal Society, was the first to mention it. In *The Newton Handbook* (London: Routledge & Kegan, 1986) by Derek Gjertsen is Stukeley's recollection of Newton's own account of the now famous apple:

> After dinner, the weather being warm, we went into the garden and drank there, under the shade of some apple trees, only he and myself. Amidst other discourse, he told me he was just in the same situation as when the notion of gravitation came into his mind. It was occassione'd by the fall of an apple, as he sat in a contemplative mood. Why should that apple always descend perpendicularly to the ground, thought he to himself. Why should it not go sideways or upwards, but constantly to the earth's center? Assuredly, the reason is the earth draws it. There must be a drawing power in matter; and the sum of the drawing power in the matter of the earth must be the earth's center. . . . If matter does draw matter, it must be in proportion of its quantity.

With the idea of gravity fixed in his mind, Newton began the task of determining the mathematics involved in universal gravitation.

During his early terms at Cambridge University, Newton was enrolled in a few mathematics courses, but he did nothing that showed his genius for mathematics. Some historians claim that when Newton left Cambridge, not even a single professor knew his name. If Newton had died of the plague, his name would be lost in the darkness of the past. Fortunately, Newton escaped the plague and lived to become one of history's greatest mathematicians.

An Apple Makes Mathematics continues on page 130.

From *Famous Problems and Their Mathematicians.* © 1999 Art Johnson. Teacher Ideas Press. (800) 237-6124.

One of the formulas Newton developed involves the distance a free-falling body travels:

$$d = 32t^2 \text{ meters}$$

In this formula, d represents the distance traveled, and t represents the number of seconds the body falls. For this activity, use Newton's formula to determine the following:

1. How many miles would you fall in 15 seconds? In 30 seconds?
2. How long would it take to fall 1 mile? 2 miles?

An Apple Makes Mathematics
Teacher Page

The solutions to the problems for the student activity are:

1. 1.4 miles, 5.5 miles

2. 12.8 seconds, 18.2 seconds

Despite the fact that Newton made such momentous discoveries, he did not publish most of them until 1687, some 20 years later. One reason for the delay was the reception Newton received when he published his findings about the nature of light. His theories were severely criticized, and he expended much time and energy defending them. Newton didn't want to do the same for his theories about calculus and universal gravitation. Consequently, he revealed his discoveries to only a few trusted colleagues. Finally, Newton's friend Sir Edmund Halley tried to convince him to publish all his findings—but Newton would only agree if Halley were to fully fund the publishing! Halley, evidently knowing what this publication would mean to the scientific community, agreed. It is also possible that Halley was in some way trying to repay Newton for his help. It was Newton who developed the mathematics that Halley used to predict the path of the great comet that now bears his name. Regardless of motivations, Halley succeeded in convincing Newton to publish his masterpiece, *The Mathematical Principles of Natural Philosophy*, in 1687.

Extension

Newton found a construction solution to an ancient Greek mathematics problem called the Delian Problem. In this problem, local priests are told by their god to enlarge a cube-shaped altar to double its volume (while still retaining the cube shape). Though this problem may seem trivial mathematically, doubling the edge length of the altar will produce a larger cube-shaped altar, but it will have eight times the volume of the original. The edge length must be increased by a factor of the cube root of 2.

Below is Newton's method for finding the edge length of the enlarged altar when given the edge length of the original altar. Ask students to use a length of 1 inch for segment AB. The resulting segment for the enlarged altar, segment AC, will have a length of the cube root of 2 inches (approximately 1.25 inches).

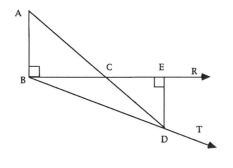

Given segment AB, construct segment BR perpendicular to segment AB. Draw segment BT such that angle ABT equals 120°. Locate point D on ray BT such that the length of segment CD equals the length of segment AB. Construct segment DE perpendicular to segment BR. Segment AC is the edge of a cube with twice the volume of a cube with segment AB as an edge. In other words, $AC^3 = 2AB^3$.

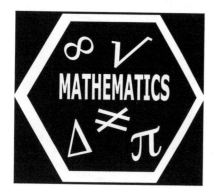

The Mysterious Mathematician

He is the mystery man of mathematics. No one knows where or when he was born. Except for the fact that he taught at the University of Alexandria, Egypt, his entire life is a complete blank. Even the year he died is unknown. Thanks to his headstone, however, we know how old he was when he died.

Diophantus (c.200–c.284), the first known algebraist, wrote extensively about algebra. All the Greek mathematicians before Diophantus wrote about either geometry or such applications of mathematics as astronomy and map-making. Only a few fragments of any of Diophantus's writings have survived to modern times. For example, his masterpiece, *Arithmetica*, originally consisted of 13 books, but only parts of six of them now exist. In *Arithmetica*, Diophantus solved various types of equations. He used a combination of words and symbols to represent these equations. The algebra symbols we use today weren't invented until more than 1,000 years after the time of Diophantus.

You might think that it isn't unusual to determine how long a person lived by looking at his or her headstone. On Diophantus's headstone, however, his age was given in a mathematics problem, presented below. For this activity, solve the problem to determine how old Diophantus was when he died.

God granted him to be a boy for the sixth part of his life, and adding a twelfth part to this, He clothed his cheeks with down; He lit him the light of marriage after a seventh part, and five years after his marriage, he granted him a son. Alas! late-born wretched child; after attaining the measure of half his father's age, chill Fate took him. After consoling his grief by this science of numbers for four years, he ended his life.

The Mysterious Mathematician
Teacher Page

For the student activity, the equation that may be written from the headstone problem is:

$$\frac{1}{6}x + \frac{1}{12}x + \frac{1}{7}x + 5 + \frac{1}{2}x + 4 = x$$

In this equation, x represents Diophantus's age at death. Solving the equation reveals that Diophantus was 84 years old when he died.

Diophantus was the first known mathematician to use symbols in mathematics. Until his equations, algebra problems were completely written in grammatical sentences called rhetorical algebra. Diophantus continued to use complete words to represent operations such as addition and subtraction, but he also used symbols to represent unknown quantities and powers of unknown quantities. This combination of words and symbols for representing algebraic equations is called syncopated algebra. Syncopated algebra, however, did not immediately affect the use of rhetorical algebra. It was not until 1500 that mathematicians again approached Diophantus's use of symbols in equations.

As a final note, Diophantus was well known to Renaissance mathematicians. It was in Claude Bachets's Latin translation of *Arithmetica* that Fermat made the notes that came to be known as Fermat's Last Theorem (see "Can It Be True?" p. 81).

Extension

Ask students to solve the following three problems from *Arithmetica*:

1. $x^2 - 4x + 4 = 0$. Solve for x. ($x = 2$)

2. Find two integers whose sum is 20 and the sum of whose squares is 208. (8, 12)

3. Find four integers such that each triple sums to 20, 22, 24, and 27. (4, 7, 9, 11)

The Witch of Agnesi

Italian mathematician Maria Gaetana Agnesi (1718–1799) is known as the Witch of Agnesi. She doesn't sound like the kind of person you'd want to meet, does she? Actually, she was nothing like a witch. She was an industrious worker and a dutiful daughter, and she cared for her younger brothers and sisters when her father died. How did she ever get stuck with the name Witch? Believe it or not, it was because of mathematics.

Agnesi was born in Bologna, Italy, the first of 21 children. She was a genius from childhood. By age nine, she could speak Italian, Latin, Greek, French, and Hebrew. At age nine, she published a paper in Latin to defend women's right to higher education. Agnesi's father, a mathematics professor, encouraged her to study mathematics along with foreign languages. By age 20, Agnesi was publishing mathematics papers. She had an unusual way of solving difficult problems. She would leave her notebook opened to the problem on her desk and go to sleep. When she woke up in the morning, the problem was solved. During the night, she would sleepwalk to her desk and solve the problem!

In 1748, Agnesi published her major work, *Instituzioni Analitiche ad Uso della Gioventu Italiana*. She began the two-volume set as a calculus text for her younger brothers and sisters, but she eventually included most of the known mathematics of her time. The books, written in a clear, simple style, were very popular, and were eventually translated into French and English. The French Academy of Science called her book "the most complete and best-written work of its kind."

In 1750, Agnesi was nominated for a full professorship at the University of Bologna by none other than Pope Benedict XVI. She was the first woman to be nominated for such a position. It was supposed that Agnesi would eventually replace her father on the faculty staff, but this was not to be. Soon after her nomination, her father became ill and died. As a result, Agnesi abandoned her pursuit of mathematics to care for all her brothers and sisters. After they grew up, she became the director of Pio Instituto Trivulo, a charitable trust for the ill and infirm, where she served for the rest of her life.

You may be wondering why she was called the Witch. She was given this name because she wrote about the curve formed by the following equation:

$$f(x) = \frac{a^3}{x^2 + a^2}$$

Through a mistranslation of Italian into English, the curve of this equation became known as "the witch," and the name became associated with Agnesi.

For this activity, use a value of 2 for *a*. Complete the table of values below and then plot the coordinate points to show the graph of the equation. Instead of plotting the points by hand, you might use a graphing calculator to find the graph.

x	f(x)
0	
1	
-1	
2	
-2	
3	
-3	
4	
-4	

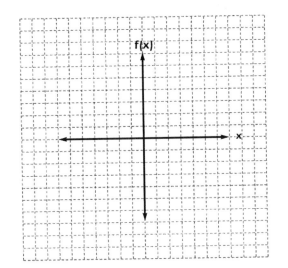

The Witch of Agnesi
Teacher Page

The graph for the student activity is as follows:

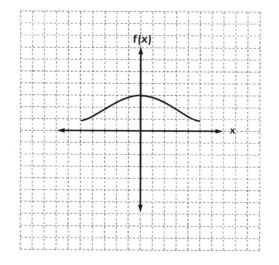

The curve that Agnesi studied was known by the term *verssoria* ("a rope that guides a sail") by Guido Grandi, the mathematician who first studied it. Agnesi included her findings about the curve in *Instituzioni Analitiche ad Uso della Gioventu Italiana*. When the text was translated into English by John Colson, he misread the word *verssoria* for the word *avversoria* ("wife of the Devil"). Since his translation, both the curve and Agnesi have been known as "witches."

Agnesi's interest in mathematics was inspired by her father. When he died in 1752, she apparently lost all interest in the field and resigned her position at the University of Bologna. In 1762, the University of Turin asked her to read and comment about the papers of a young mathematician named Joseph LaGrange. She responded that she was "no longer concerned with such interests."

Extension

Have students graph "the witch" using other values for a, such as 3 and 5. Have them explain how changing the value of a changes the curve. A graphing calculator is helpful for this activity.

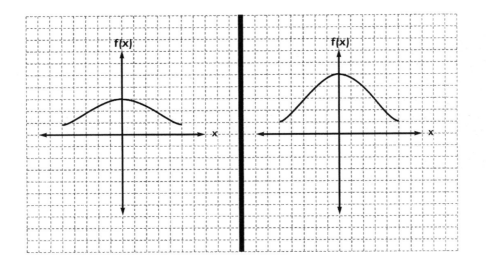

$a = 3 \quad a = 5$

As the value of a increases, the y-intercept, or $f(x)$-intercept, of the curve increases.

"Let No One Ignorant of Geometry Enter Here!"

That's what the sign said. It was placed above the entrance so everyone could see it. What did it mean? Why did Plato (c.429–c.348 B.C.), a famous Greek philosopher, put this sign at the entrance to his famous school? What message was he trying to send?

Plato is not known for his mathematics. He wrote about philosophy, ethics, religion, and politics. At the academy where he taught, he helped his students to reason about such things and to ponder the very meaning of life itself. He did not plan to teach them any geometry, or even mathematics. Why then the sign? Plato used the sign because he wanted students who could reason, form conclusions, and follow logical arguments. This is the kind of thinking used in mathematics, especially in geometry. Plato thought that if his students had mastered geometry, they must have also developed the rigorous thinking process that was essential for learning the philosophy he wanted to teach at the academy.

Plato did write about mathematics in some of his books. For example, in *Meno*, the main character, Meno, must draw a square that has twice the area of a given square. In other words, given square *ABCD* below, he must construct a new square, *QRST*, that has twice the area of square *ABCD*.

How would you solve such a problem? If you double the side lengths of square *ABCD*, the resulting square *QRST* has four times the area of square *ABCD*:

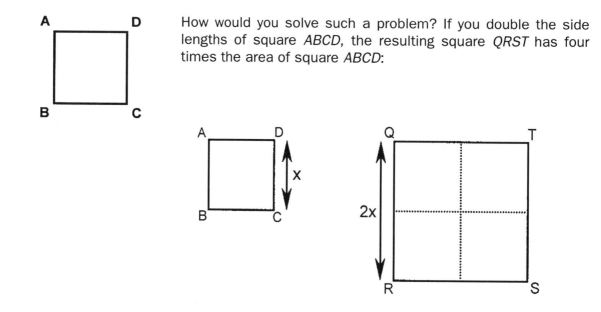

This was the problem Meno faced. Can you solve the problem? For this activity, draw square *QRST* below such that it has twice the area of square *ABCD*.

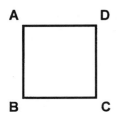

"Let No One Ignorant of Geometry Enter Here!"
Teacher Page

In *Meno*, the problem of doubling a square's area in a new square is discussed in a dialogue between the slave Meno and Socrates, the famous Greek philosopher. Socrates leads Meno to the conclusion that the enlarged square may be constructed by using the diagonal of the original square, square *ABCD*, as a side of the enlarged square, square *QRST*.

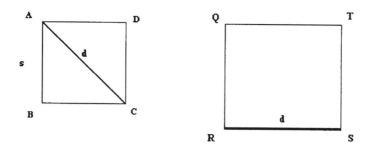

This method makes use of the relationship between the side, s, and diagonal, d, of a square:

$$d = s\sqrt{2}$$

That the area of square *QRST* is twice the area of square *ABCD* can be verified mathematically:

Area of square $ABCD = s^2$

Area of square $QRST = d^2 = (s\sqrt{2})^2 = 2s^2$

One way to verify the actual construction is to divide square *QRST* using its two diagonals. The resulting four right triangles each have half the area of the original square. Thus, square *QRST* has twice the area of square *ABCD*.

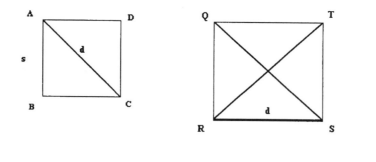

Like Plato, Socrates was a philosopher. He was Plato's teacher, just as Plato was Aristotle's teacher. Plato is the only source of information we have about Socrates. There is no other evidence that Socrates even existed. For this reason, some have suggested that Socrates was a fictitious character invented by Plato to embody all the qualities that a good teacher should possess. Fictitious or not, the questioning method used by Socrates to teach Meno, called the Socratic Method, continues to be a model for educators today.

Plato also described the five regular polyhedrons: the tetrahedron (4 triangular faces), cube (6 square faces), octahedron (8 triangular faces), dodecahedron (12 pentagonal faces), and icosahedron (20 triangular faces). They are called Platonic Solids, although Plato did not discover them. Plato used these polyhedrons to explain his understanding of the universe. For Plato, the tetrahedron represented fire, the cube represented the earth, the octahedron represented air, and the icosahedron represented water. Plato thought that the dodecahedron was the most perfect solid, so it represented the entire universe.

Extension

Plato discovered a formula for generating Pythagorean Triples, or integer values for the three sides of a right triangle:

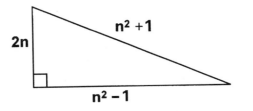

Have students generate Pythagorean Triples using the following values for n (the values should be rounded to the nearest integer):

1. Age

2. House or apartment number

3. Shoe size

4. Birth date (day of the month)

5. Height in inches

The Disappointed Daughter

When most mathematicians write a book about mathematics, they give it a title that describes the contents of the book. Bhaskara Acharya (1114–1185), the last great Hindu mathematician of the Middle Ages, did not. He named his life's work *Lilavati* after his daughter. He did it to comfort her. What happened to Lilavati that caused her father to title his greatest book after her?

Bhaskara was not only a mathematician but also an astrologer. To ensure a happy marriage for his daughter, he determined the exact day and hour for his daughter's wedding. Bhaskara insisted that any other day or hour would be unfavorable. On the day of the wedding, his daughter anxiously checked the water clock every few minutes so she would be ready for the eventful time. During one of her checks, a pearl fell from her headdress into the water clock and clogged the timing hole. Before anyone realized what had happened, the hour determined by her father had passed. There would be no wedding for Lilavati—not then, not ever. Her time had passed. We don't know if having her father's book named after her made Lilavati feel any better, but her name became known throughout the world.

Three of the problems from the book *Lilavati* are presented below. For this activity, solve any two of them.

1. If a bamboo 32 cubits high is broken by the wind so the tip meets the ground 16 cubits from the base, at what height was it broken?

2. The eighth portion of a troop of monkeys, squared, was skipping in a grove and delighted in their sport. Twelve remaining monkeys were seen on a hill, amused with chattering to each other. How many monkeys were there in all?

3. The mixed price of 9 citrons and 7 fragrant wood apples is 107; again the mixed price of 7 citrons and 9 fragrant wood apples is 101. O, you arithmetician, tell me quickly the price of a citron and a wood apple, having distinctly separated those prices as well.

The Disappointed Daughter
Teacher Page

The solutions to the problems for the student activity are:

1. 12 cubits

2. 16 or 48 monkeys

3. Price of a citron is 8; price of a fragrant wood apple is 5

Bhaskara filled *Lilavati* with a compilation of previously existing problems, along with some of his own. The bamboo problem (with different data) was proposed by fellow Hindu mathematician Brahmagupta some 50 years earlier, and was especially popular in China. It appears in a book by Ch'ang Ts'ang written about 200 B.C.

Bhaskara also wrote about the mathematics of zero. Although the concept of zero was discovered and in common use years before Bhaskara's time (the earliest written form of zero is on a wall of a temple in Gvalior, India, which dates to 840), some claim that Bhaskara was the first mathematician to fully understand the implications of using zero in computations. In *Vija-Ganita* ("Root Calculations"), Bhaskara suggests, for example, that $3/0$ results in an infinite quantity, not zero. However, he also suggests that $3/0 \times 0 = 3$, thus indicating that he still had not fully developed the modern concept of zero.

Extension

The shortest proof in the history of mathematics is found in *Vija-Ganita*. It is a proof of the Pythagorean Theorem:

Bhaskara's original diagram did not show the lengths of the sides as a, b, and c. These variables will be helpful to students for this extension. Present Bhaskara's proof to students and ask them to explain how his diagram proves the Pythagorean Theorem.

The areas of the figures prove the Pythagorean Theorem as follows:

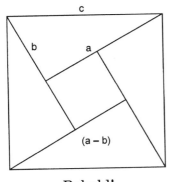

Behold!

Area of large square	=	Area of four right triangles + area of small square
c^2	=	$4(\dfrac{ab}{2}) + (a-b)^2$
c^2	=	$2ab + (a^2 - 2ab + b^2)$
c^2	=	$a^2 + b^2$

From *Famous Problems and Their Mathematicians.* © 1999 Art Johnson. Teacher Ideas Press. (800) 237-6124.

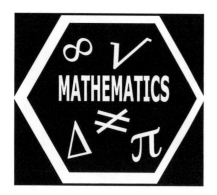

Unfulfilled Promise

German mathematician Johann Müller (1436–1476), also known as Regiomontanus, had finally reached the height of fame. He had been invited to Rome by the pope himself. Pope Sixus IV had asked Regiomontanus to come to Rome to help revise the calendar, which was now in serious need of updating. Regiomontanus was just the person for the job. He was the best known mathematician of his time, and astronomical studies were his specialty. When he was only 13, Regiomontanus attended the University of Leipzig. He later attended and then taught at the University of Vienna. Eventually, he was appointed court astronomer to King Matthias Corvinus of Hungary.

Regiomontanus was certain he could use his knowledge about the movements of the sun and the moon to easily devise a more accurate calendar. When he finished the job, he would certainly earn the gratitude of the pope. Who knew what might happen next? As a trusted advisor to the pope, Regiomontanus would have great influence and power for years to come. He was a young man, only 39. In the right circumstances, he himself might even become pope someday!

It was not to be. Regiomontanus died within a year after going to Rome. The official cause of death was the plague, but persistent rumors suggest he was poisoned. Who would want to poison a mathematician? Regiomontanus was German, and his enemies most likely feared he would gain too much influence with the pope. They wanted to ensure that the pope and the papal court remained Italian. A life full of promise, with a glorious future, was thus cut short. Some historians speculate that if Regiomontanus had lived a full life, he might have been the one who developed our modern understanding of the solar system, instead of Copernicus about 100 years later.

Regiomontanus has been called the first modern European mathematician. This is because he understood the purpose of mathematics to include more than simple arithmetic applications. In addition to writing about astronomical movements, he also wrote about trigonometry and geometry. He was the greatest mathematician of his century.

Regiomontanus's most famous book is *De Triangulus Omnimodes*, which he wrote in 1464. In *De Triangulus*, Regiomontanus presents a modern view of trigonometry and data tables for the various trigonometric functions. The following problem is from *De Triangulus*:

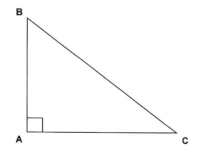

For this activity, try to solve Regiomontanus's problem. In triangle *ABC*, the ratio of angle *A* to angle *B* is 10:7, and the ratio of angle *B* to angle *C* is 7:3. Solve for all three angles of triangle *ABC*.

Unfulfilled Promise
Teacher Page

The solution of the problem for the student activity is: angle A = 90°, angle B = 63°, and angle C = 27°.

In *De Triangulus*, Regiomontanus devised trigonometric tables that contained no fractions. Because this book was written before the concept of decimal notation was developed, fractions were a tedious but necessary part of trigonometry problems. By using a circle with a radius of 100,000,000 units to compute the values of his trigonometric tables, Regiomontanus produced integer values. *De Triangulus* greatly influenced all who read it, but its audience was narrow. Until it was typeset in 1533, only a few manuscript copies circulated throughout Europe.

Regiomontanus adopted his name from the city where he was born, Konigsberg, Prussia. The word *Konigsberg* means "King's Mountain," for which *Regiomontanus* is the Latinized word.

Extension

An interesting problem from the writings of Regiomontanus is one that asks where to stand for the best view of a painting on a wall. If you stand too close, you distort the upper portion. If you stand too far from the painting, well, you are too far back and cannot see all the details of the painting. The following diagram illustrates the problem situation:

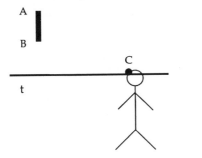

The painting on the wall is represented by segment AB, and the eye height of the person viewing the painting is represented by point C. Line t is a horizontal line drawn through point C.

Regiomontanus found that when a circle is constructed so that it is tangent to line t and intersects points A and B, the point of tangency of the circle and line t (point Q) is the best viewing point for the painting:

Share this information with your students and have them find the best viewing point for a poster in the classroom.

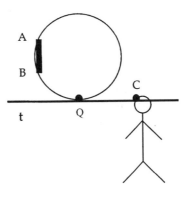

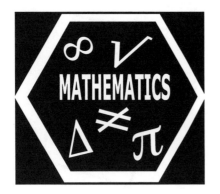

The Artist As Mathematician

Leonardo da Vinci (1452–1519) was one of the outstanding figures of the Renaissance. He is known the world over as the artist of two of the most famous paintings of all time—*The Mona Lisa* and *The Last Supper*. Leonardo was more than an artist, though. He explored medicine, biology, optics, astronomy, physics, archeology, mechanics, anatomy, and botany. He proposed an ultramodern city with subterranean travel passages and a sewage system. Leonardo also designed weapons of war, including tanks, submarines, parachutes, and even a helicopter. It seems there was no limit to his wide-ranging interests.

Late in life, Leonardo recalled an event from his youth that provided a hint to his broad interests as an adult. He remembered finding a cave near his home one day. Leonardo stood outside the cave, alone, trying to overcome his fear of the dark so he could explore it. He finally did, "prompted by the desire to see whether there might be any marvelous things within." It seems that Leonardo's entire life was dedicated to discovering "marvelous things." Leonardo carried his discoveries into his personal life. He had such a reverence for living things that he frequently bought caged birds at the market place so he could set them free. His study of anatomy convinced him to become a vegetarian and to drink wine only on rare occasions.

Leonardo also made discoveries in mathematics. He said, "There is no certainty in science where mathematics cannot be applied." One of his discoveries involves the following diagram:

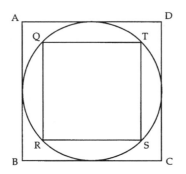

Square *ABCD* is circumscribed about a circle (that is, each side of square *ABCD* is tangent to the circle). Square *QRST* is inscribed in the circle (that is, the four vertices of square *QRST* are on the circle). For this activity, explain how the area of square *ABCD* compares to the area of square *QRST*.

The Artist As Mathematician Teacher Page

Leonardo expressed his discovery regarding the problem for the student activity as follows: "When each of two squares touch the same circle at four points, one is double the other." In the diagram, square $ABCD$ has a side length equal to twice the radius, r, of the circle. Square $QRST$ has a side length (s) of $r\sqrt{2}$. (In triangle QRS, $s^2 + s^2 = (2r)^2$ and $s = r\sqrt{2}$.)

Area of square $ABCD = (2r)^2 = 4r^2$

Area of square $QRST = (r\sqrt{2})^2 = 2r^2$

Thus, the larger square, square $ABCD$, has twice the area of the smaller square, square $QRST$.

Although Leonardo is well known as an artist, he produced only 17 paintings during his entire career. Early in his life, he was interested only in his art, but as he grew older, he became more interested in other pursuits. For the last two decades of his life, Leonardo focused on scientific explorations and experimentations and gave his art limited attention. In 1504, a friend wrote, "He (Leonardo) is working hard at geometry and is increasingly impatient with his paint brush. . . . In short, his mathematical explorations have distracted him so much from painting that he can no longer stand his paint brush."

The time period during which Leonardo lived was not conducive to his explorations. For example, he studied anatomy by performing autopsies—a total of 30 by his count. When news of this reached the pope, he forbade Leonardo access to either a hospital or a mortuary for the rest of his life. Leonardo also wrote his notebooks in mirror image, from right to left. Some have suggested he did so to make his notes illegible to the casual reader, who might misconstrue the goals of his many experiments. Although writing in mirror image may seem to be a difficult task, Leonardo was an artist, and left-handed at that, so for him this was quite easy.

Multitalented Leonardo was not alone in pursuing both art and science during the Renaissance. Many artists were also scientists or mathematicians, or both. Albrecht Dürer was a German artist who wrote extensively about the mathematics of perspective. Michaelangelo, in addition to being a painter and sculptor, was the chief architect of St. Peter's Basilica in Rome. The design of this basilica required an artist's eye and an architect's vision.

The Artist As Mathematician Teacher Page continues on page 148.

Extension

Much of Leonardo's writings involved practical application of mathematics. Present the following problem, which is typical of the practical problems that Leonardo developed, to students and have them solve it.

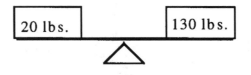

A 20-pound weight and a 130-pound weight must be balanced at opposite ends of a 20-foot beam. How far must the balancing point (fulcrum) be placed from the 20-pound weight?

The problem may be solved as follows:

$$\text{weight}_1 \times \text{distance}_1 = \text{weight}_2 \times \text{distance}_2$$

$$20x = 130(20 - x)$$

$$x = 17.3 \text{ feet} = 17 \text{ feet, 4 inches}$$

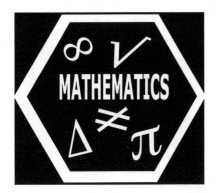

To the Highest Bidder

Today, outstanding professional athletes are in great demand. They are offered contracts of millions of dollars for their talents. There was a time when the same was true for outstanding mathematicians. Well, maybe not the contracts for millions of dollars, but certainly about mathematicians being in great demand. Italian mathematician Vincenzo Viviani (1622–1703) was one of those who profited from the great demand for mathematicians.

In 1666, Viviani was a member of the court of the Grand Duke of Tuscany in Florence, Italy. In that same year, he received an offer from Louis XIV of France to become a mathematician for the Royal Academy, and also an offer from King John II Casimir of Poland to be his official Court Astronomer. He told the grand duke about the offers and received a promotion to Court Mathematician and a substantial increase in pay.

Even as a young student, Viviani possessed an outstanding ability in mathematics. He studied with the two greatest Italian scientists/mathematicians of the day, Galileo and Torricelli. Viviani's mathematics involved practical applications and engineering topics. In 1660, he determined the speed of sound by timing the flash and sound of a cannon. His finding was within 10% of the actual speed, a significant improvement over the previously computed speed, which was 45% in error.

Viviani discovered an interesting property about a random point in any equilateral triangle. He found that if segments are drawn from the random point perpendicular to the sides of the equilateral triangle, the sum of the lengths of the three segments is equal to the length of a specific segment of the triangle.

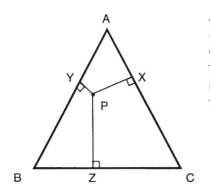

For this activity, draw several different equilateral triangles, *ABC*, and locate a point, *P*, at a different location inside each triangle. Draw segments *PX*, *PY*, and *PZ* such that they are perpendicular to the sides of the triangle. Use your diagrams and a ruler to determine whether the sum of the lengths of these three segments is equal to the length of a side, the length of an altitude, or the length of a median in an equilateral triangle.

To the Highest Bidder
Teacher Page

Viviani found that the sum of the lengths of the three segments is equal to the length of an altitude. This result may be found using dynamic geometry software. It also may be shown by the following diagram:

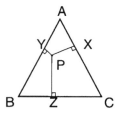

In this diagram, as point P approaches the position of vertex A, segment PZ approaches the position and the length of the altitude from point A, while the other two segments, PX and PY, become increasingly shorter. Eventually, the lengths of segments PX and PY become zero, and the length of segment PZ becomes equal to the length of the altitude from point A.

A formal proof is based on the fact that the sum of the areas of APB, BPC, and CPA is equal to the area of ABC:

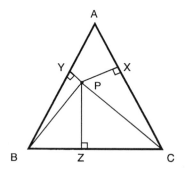

Area APB + Area BPC + Area CPA = Area ABC

$$\tfrac{1}{2}(AB \times PY) + \tfrac{1}{2}(BC \times PZ) + \tfrac{1}{2}(AC \times PX) = \tfrac{1}{2}(BC \times \text{altitude from point } A)$$

Because sides of an equilateral triangle are congruent, substitute BC for AB and AC:

$$\tfrac{1}{2}(BC \times PY) + \tfrac{1}{2}(BC \times PZ) + \tfrac{1}{2}(BC \times PX) = \tfrac{1}{2}(BC \times \text{altitude from point } A)$$

$$\tfrac{1}{2}BC(PY + PZ + PX) = \tfrac{1}{2}BC(\text{altitude from point } A)$$

$$PY + PZ + PX = \text{Altitude from point } A$$

It is surprising that this theorem was not discovered by the ancient Greeks. The theorem and its proof are within the understanding of most students with a basic knowledge of geometry.

French mathematician Pierre Varignon (1654–1722), a contemporary of Viviani's, also discovered a fairly simple geometric relationship. Varignon's theorem involves a random quadrilateral $ABCD$, with midpoints $Q, R, S,$ and T. When these midpoints are connected, the resulting midpoint quadrilateral is always a parallelogram, as shown in the following figure:

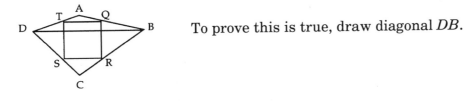 To prove this is true, draw diagonal DB.

In triangle ADB, TQ is a midline, thus: $\quad TQ \parallel DB \qquad TQ = \frac{1}{2}DB$

In triangle CDB, SR is a midline, thus: $\quad SR \parallel DB \qquad SR = \frac{1}{2}DB$

Thus, $TQ \parallel SR$, and $TQ = SR$. Therefore, quadrilateral $QRST$ must be a parallelogram.

Extension

Have students investigate midpoint quadrilaterals for various quadrilaterals to determine which parallelograms are rhombuses or squares. Supply the following table, with only the first midpoint quadrilateral identified, and ask students to complete it.

Initial Quadrilateral	Midpoint Quadrilateral
Random quadrilateral	parallelogram
Parallelogram	(parallelogram)
Rectangle	(rhombus)
Rhombus	(rectangle)
Square	(square)
Trapezoid	(parallelogram)
Isosceles trapezoid	(rhombus)

Great Potential

A philosopher once said that there is no heavier burden than having great potential. What he meant is that few people who have great potential ever meet it. Sometimes, they only disappoint themselves, their family, and their friends. One mathematician who showed great potential at an early age was Charles Julien Branchion (1785–1864). He was an outstanding mathematics student who attended the famous École Polytechnique, where he was taught by Gaspard Monge (1746–1818), a well-known mathematics professor. After only one year of study with Monge, Branchion made the discovery that became known as Branchion's Theorem.

With such an accomplishment at only 19, Branchion had great potential. He never managed to achieve it, though. He advanced a new geometry, called projective geometry, but it never equaled the success of his theorem. Branchion's Theorem states, "If a hexagon is circumscribed about a conic section, then the diagonals which join opposite points are concurrent."

For this activity, find out what concurrent diagonals are by following these steps:

1. Draw hexagon *QRSTUV* around the circle so that each side of the hexagon touches the circle at only one point.

2. Draw diagonals *QT*, *RU*, and *SV*.

What do you notice about the three diagonals you have drawn?

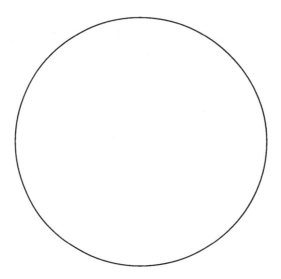

Great Potential
Teacher Page

The following is a diagram of Branchion's Theorem:

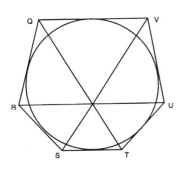

As this diagram shows, the diagonals of any hexagon circumscribed about a conic section will have concurrent diagonals joining opposite vertices. In this diagram, the hexagon is circumscribed about a circle, but a hexagon can also be circumscribed about any other conic section—parabola, hyperbola, or ellipse—to produce the same result.

Branchion's adult life was not completely without accomplishment. He is credited with collaborating on the Nine-Point Circle with college classmate Jean Victor Poncelet. However, he never again approached the originality and vision of the theorem that bears his name.

Another mathematician who showed great promise at a young age was Blaise Pascal (1623–1662). Pascal was only 14 when he was invited to join the weekly meetings of the outstanding mathematicians of the day, held at Marin Mersenne's house in Paris. By all accounts, young Pascal was an equal participant in the discussions that took place. At age 16, Pascal made a discovery that drew the attention of mathematicians everywhere. His discovery was so outstanding for one so young that René Descartes, one of the mathematicians whom Pascal met at Mersenne's meetings, refused to believe that Pascal was responsible for the discovery and its proof. Pascal's discovery was this: "If a hexagon with no parallel sides is inscribed in a conic section, then the three intersection points of the three opposite sides will be collinear."

This discovery was the first of many. Pascal continued to advance his mathematical knowledge, and made many other contributions to mathematics in the fields of geometry and probability. Along with Fermat, Pascal is considered the Co-Father of Probability Theory. Truly, Pascal reached his great potential.

Extension

Ask students to follow the directions below to make a sketch representing Pascal's theorem, which he called the Mystic Hexagram. Stress to students that not only should opposite sides not be parallel, but they should not even be close to parallel. If students draw a hexagon with opposite sides that are close to parallel, their resulting Mystic Hexagram will not fit on a regular sheet of paper.

Great Potential Teacher Page continues on page 154.

1. Inscribe hexagon *ABCDEF* in a circle.
2. Label the intersection of line *AB* and line *DE* as point *L*.
3. Label the intersection of line *DC* and line *AF* as point *M*.
4. Label the intersection of line *EF* and line *BC* as point *N*.

As discovered by Pascal, points *L*, *M*, and *N* are collinear.

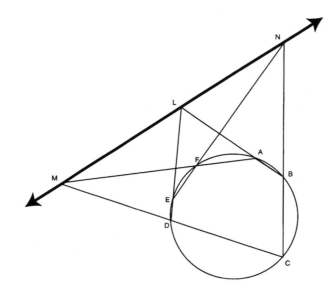

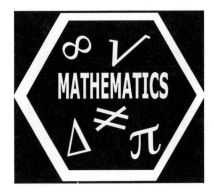

Mathematics As a Religion

He was trapped. The mob was approaching, and there was no escape. Unless . . . unless he ran across a farmer's field planted with beans. If he did that, he could hide in the thicket on the other side of the field and then escape. No! He couldn't do that. It would be against all his principles. So, according to some historians, Greek mathematician Pythagoras (c.570–c.500 B.C.) met an untimely death because he had refused to run across a field of beans. Why was crossing a field of beans against his principles?

Pythagoras is a near legendary figure in the history of mathematics. He believed that numbers and mathematics held mystical and religious properties. Pythagoras gathered a number of followers, who devoted themselves to him and his teachings—and what teachings they were! Because they believed in reincarnation, the Pythagoreans were vegetarians who refused to wear wool or leather clothing. The Pythagorean belief in reincarnation held that when a person died, his or her soul traveled and was reborn into another living being, sometimes human, sometimes animal. Thus, wearing leather or wool might mean wearing part of a person you once knew. A Pythagorean certainly wouldn't eat an animal, because it might house the soul of a departed friend or family member. One tale about Pythagoras illustrates his belief in reincarnation: Pythagoras came upon a man beating a dog, and moved to save the dog. Why? Pythagoras had recognized the dog's cries to be the voice of a recently departed friend!

Why wouldn't Pythagoras cross the field of beans? Some beans resemble an unborn baby. For Pythagoras, these beans were the temporary resting place of the soul on its journey to becoming another being. A person running across a field of beans might accidentally crush one of these resting souls. Such unusual beliefs made Pythagoras suspicious to the average citizen. In addition, he refused to believe in the gods the Greeks worshipped. It's no wonder he was chased by a mob of angry people.

Pythagoras is best known for the Pythagorean Theorem: In a right triangle, the sum of the squares of the two legs is equal to the square of the hypotenuse.

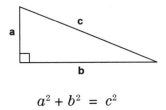

$$a^2 + b^2 = c^2$$

Mathematics As a Religion continues on page 156.

155

Although the theorem carries Pythagoras's name, he was not the first to use it. Forms of the Pythagorean Theorem have been found in earlier Babylonian, Egyptian, and Chinese writings. In fact, Pythagoras may not have even discovered the theorem by himself. Some claim that his followers were so devoted to Pythagoras that they gave him the credit for all their discoveries. Perhaps the Pythagorean Theorem might be better called the Unknown Follower Theorem!

Mathematics historians suggest that the Pythagoreans' proof of the Pythagorean Theorem might have involved the following diagram:

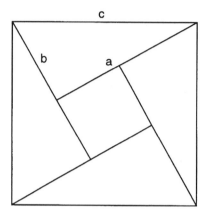

For this activity, trace the diagram above and cut out the five shapes of this $c \times c$ square. Rearrange the shapes to form two smaller squares: an $a \times a$ square and a $b \times b$ square. (Hint: The two squares are parts of one arrangement of all five pieces.) Can you explain how these two smaller squares prove the Pythagorean Theorem?

Mathematics As a Religion
Teacher Page

If the five pieces of the diagram are arranged as shown below, they form an $a \times a$ square and a $b \times b$ square. Thus, $a^2 + b^2 = c^2$.

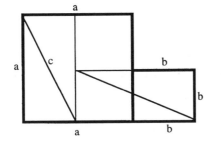

There are literally hundreds of proofs of the Pythagorean Theorem. *The Pythagorean Proposition* (1968) by Elisha Scott Loomis presents 256 proofs by a wide range of people. Some of the mathematicians who discovered proofs for the Pythagorean Theorem are Newton, Omar Al-Khayyam, Galileo, Copernicus, Diogenes, Socrates, Plato, President Garfield, and even a number of high school students.

Extension

The great Renaissance painter Leonardo da Vinci explored mathematics. One of his achievements was an original proof of the Pythagorean Theorem. Present Leonardo's diagram, below, to your students and ask them to use it to show that $a^2 + b^2 = c^2$.

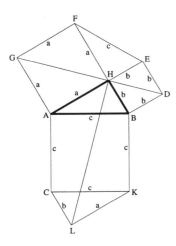

In this diagram, squares are constructed off the sides of right triangle AHB. Triangle AHB is congruent to triangle FHE by side-angle-side (SAS). Triangle KLC is constructed congruent to triangle AHB. Quadrilateral GFED is congruent to qualrilateral LKBH by side-angle-side-angle-side (SASAS). Thus, the area of hexagon ABDEFG equals the area of hexagon AHBKLC. If the areas of triangle AHB and FHE are subtracted from hexagon ABDEFG, and the areas of triangles AHB and KLC are subtracted from hexagon AHBKLC, then the area of square GAHF ($a \times a = a^2$) plus the area of square HEDB ($b \times b = b^2$) equals the area of square ACKB ($c \times c = c^2$). In other words, $a^2 + b^2 = c^2$.

In this diagram, triangles *EFH*, *ABH*, and *CKL* are congruent. The two hexagons, *AHBKLC* and *ABDEFG*, are equal in area. By subtracting the area of triangles *EFH* and *CKL* from the areas of the hexagons, square *ABCK* (with a side length of *c*) is equal in area to the sum of the areas of squares *AHFG* (with a side length of *a*) and *BDEH* (with a side length of *b*). Thus, $a^2 + b^2 = c^2$.

The Lineup

At first glance, it doesn't look like much—just a few intersecting lines. There is more to it than meets the eye, though. David Hilbert (1862–1943), the greatest mathematician of the twentieth century, called it "the most important figure in mathematics." What was it? A delicate design? A complex equation? It was a simple construction by ancient Greek mathematician Pappus (c.290–c.350).

Pappus was the last of the great Greek mathematicians. His major work was *The Mathematical Collection* or, simply, *The Collection*—an apt name. It was a collection of all the mathematics that had been discovered up to the time Pappus lived. In the eight books of *The Collection*, Pappus wrote summaries and explanations of more than 25 mathematicians' work, including Euclid, Archimedes, Eratosthenes, and Appolonius. The topics included are area, volume, spirals, solids, arithmetic, and mechanics. *The Collection* included everything. It wasn't meant to be an encyclopedia, but rather a "handbook" that would help a reader with the original writings of other mathematicians. Pappus included some of his own discoveries, too. One of these is known as Pappus's Theorem.

Pappus's Theorem concerns points on two nonparallel lines. Pappus made a conclusion about the intersection points of the segments that connect the points on the nonparallel lines. For this activity, follow the directions below to discover Pappus's Theorem. When you have completed the construction, you will be able to see "the most important figure in mathematics."

1. Label the intersection of line *AR* and line *QB* as point *X*.

2. Label the intersection of line *AS* and line *QC* as point *Y*.

3. Label the intersection of line *BS* and line *RC* as point *Z*.

What do you notice about the three points *X*, *Y*, and *Z*?

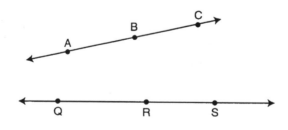

The Lineup
Teacher Page

The result of the students activity is as follows:

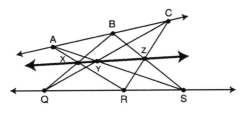

Points X, Y, and Z are collinear. Most students should be able to make a conjecture about Pappus's Theorem from their construction. Pappus proved that the intersection points of these three pairs of segments are always collinear, and Hilbert understood this discovery to be a mathematics milestone.

Pappus was the last Greek mathematician who did original work of any consequence. It is true that he was followed by Hypatia and Proclus, but most mathematics historians think that Pappus's death signaled the end of the era of Greek mathematics.

Extension

Joseph-Dias Gergonne (1771–1859) is also known for a geometric construction. Gergonne was an officer in an artillery corps, as well as a mathematician who helped develop the field of projective geometry. He initiated the first private periodical in mathematics, *Annales de Gergonne*, in 1810. The title *Annales de Gergonne* is misleading because many other mathematicians published articles in *Annales*, including Poncelet, Monge, and Galois. Gergonne's construction is known as Gergonne's Point, and involves a point inside a circle.

Ask your students to locate Gergonne's Point by following these directions:

1. Inscribe a circle in an acute, scalene triangle ABC.

2. Label the points where the triangle is tangent to the circle X, Y, and Z, respectively. That is, point X lies on segment AB, point Y lies on segment BC, and point Z lies on segment CA.

The Lineup Teacher Page continues on page 160.

---

3. Draw cevians from each vertex of the triangle to the opposite tangent point. That is, draw segments *AY*, *BZ*, and *CX*.
    (The term *cevian* was named after the Italian mathematician who first employed it in his mathematics, Giovanni Ceva. A cevian is a segment drawn from the vertex of a triangle to any point on the opposite side. It is the only term in geometry that originates from a mathematician's name.)

4. Find Gergonne's Point, the point of concurrency of segments *AY*, *BZ*, and *CX*.

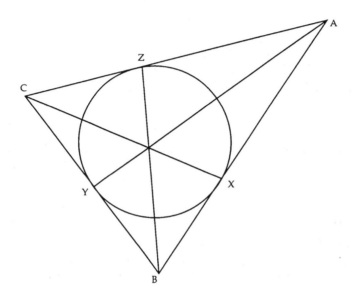

The Politician As Mathematician

Everyone has heard of Napoleon Bonaparte (1769–1821), the great military strategist and emperor of France. He was also a brilliant mathematics student. Did you know that with everything else he accomplished in his life, he also discovered a geometry theorem that is named after him?

Napoleon was the top mathematics student in his public school in Brienne, France, where he studied algebra, trigonometry, and geometry. After he graduated, Napoleon applied to the Paris Military Academy. Although he had average abilities in other subjects, Napoleon excelled in mathematics. It was his mathematical ability that gained him admittance to the academy. Once enrolled, Napoleon continued to impress his instructors and his classmates with his genius in mathematics. Eventually, mathematicians were drawn to Napoleon, and one of them, Lorenzo Mascheroni (1750–1800), even dedicated a book to him.

When Napoleon led a military campaign to Egypt in 1798, he took with him a number of educators, including mathematicians Gaspard Monge (1746–1818) and Joseph Fourier (1768–1830). After he became emperor, Napoleon placed Monge, Fourier, and other mathematicians in influential positions in his government. Their mission was to create new schools, restructure the educational system, and recruit new teachers. They were also expected to emphasize mathematics in the school curriculum. To this day, mathematics is one of the central topics in French schools.

The theorem Napoleon discovered is called, appropriately, Napoleon's Theorem. For this activity, follow the directions below to demonstrate Napoleon's Theorem.

1. Construct an equilateral triangle on each side of triangle *ABC*. Label the three equilateral triangles *ABX*, *BCY*, and *ACZ*.

2. Construct the common point of the angle bisectors of the three angles in each equilateral triangle. Label the common point in triangle *ABX* as point *Q*, the common point in triangle *BCY* as point *R*, and the common point in triangle *ACZ* as point *S*.

3. Draw triangle *QRS*.

What do you think Napoleon's Theorem states about triangle *QRS*? Write a statement.

The Politician As Mathematician Teacher Page

The diagram below shows that triangle QRS is equilateral. Although Napoleon was not the first to discover this, he is credited with finding and proving the theorem, and so it is named after him. There are some mathematics historians who claim that the mathematics necessary for discovering and proving this theorem was beyond the ability of Napoleon. Regardless, it is now known as Napoleon's Theorem by his admirers and critics alike. If students draw segment XC, segment YA, and segment ZB in their construction, they will find that the segments are concurrent. They meet at a point called Napoleon's Point.

Extension

One politician who did make an original contribution to mathematics was President James A. Garfield (1831–1881), who was elected president in 1880. Some five years earlier, when he was a member of the House of Representatives, Garfield discovered a proof of the Pythagorean Theorem, shown below.

Present the diagram of the proof, below, to your students. Ask them to use the diagram to prove $a^2 + b^2 = c^2$, as Garfield did. You might give students the hint to use the areas of the figures for their proof.

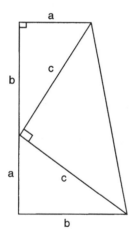

In the diagram, three right triangles are combined to form a trapezoid. The sum of the areas of the three right triangles is equal to the area of the trapezoid:

Area of trapezoid	=	Area of three right triangles
$\frac{1}{2}(a + b)(a + b)$	=	$\frac{1}{2}ab + \frac{1}{2}ab + \frac{1}{2}c^2$
$(a + b)(a + b)$	=	$ab + ab + c^2$
$a^2 + 2ab + b^2$	=	$2ab + c^2$
$a^2 + b^2$	=	c^2

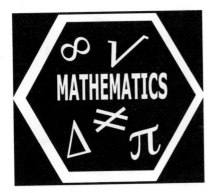

MATHEMATICS

The Poet As Mathematician

Suppose the governor of your state promised to help you in any way possible. What would you ask the governor to do for you? That's what happened to Persian mathematician and poet Omar Al-Khayyam (1044–1130). What do you think he asked for?

Al-Khayyam lived at the height of Islamic development in mathematics. He was the first mathematician to categorize all 13 types of cubic equations. In his book *Maqalat fi Al-Jabr wa Al-Muqabila*, Al-Khayyam used the intersections of conic sections to find the positive roots of these complex equations. He also wrote about Euclid's geometry and specific gravity.

In 1074, he was summoned by Sultan Malikshah Jalal al-Din to design a more accurate calendar. The existing calendar contained inaccuracies that affected tax collections and the observance of holy days. Al-Khayyam designed a new calendar that required eight leap years every 33 years. His calendar was more accurate than the one we use today. Our calendar requires an extra day every 3,330 years, while Al-Khayyam's calendar requires an extra day every 3,770 years.

What about Al-Khayyam's decision? It all began as a pact between boys. Al-Khayyam and his two childhood friends, Nizam-al-Mulk and Hassan Ben Sabbath, agreed that if any one of them became successful in life, he would grant the other two any favor in his power. When Nizam-al-Mulk became a vizier, a high government official, to Sultan Alp Arslan, Hassan Ben Sabbath asked him for an influential government position, which Nizam-al-Mulk granted. Al-Khayyam simply asked for a modest yearly salary to allow him to focus on his mathematics and his poetry.

Who made the best choice? Eventually, Hassan Ben Sabbath tried to overthrow the provincial government and was removed from office. He fled to the mountains and, later, led a band of fanatics who preyed on caravans that passed their stronghold near the Caspian Sea. One passing caravan was led by his old friend Nizam-al-Mulk. Hassan Ben Sabbath's band attacked the caravan and killed his boyhood friend. Hassan Ben Sabbath was ultimately caught and executed for his crimes.

Al-Khayyam's two friends died untimely deaths, while Al-Khayyam lived a long life, winning fame and respect for his great learning and the beauty of his poetry. Al-Khayyam is actually better known as a poet than as a mathematician. He composed the *Rubaiyat*, a collection of beautiful verses with elaborate and detailed images. The *Rubaiyat* is one of the most outstanding poems produced by any culture.

Many Islamic mathematicians focused on problems of inheritance because the Koran has very specific rules about how wealth is to be passed on to surviving family members. The following problem is from the writings of another Islamic mathematician, Al-Khwarizimi. For this activity, solve the problem to determine how the inheritance is to be divided.

> If a man dies, leaving no children, his mother receives 1/6 of the estate and his widow 1/4. If he has any brothers or sisters, a brother's share is twice that of a sister's. Find the fractions of the estate due if a man dies, leaving no children and no mother, but leaving a wife, a brother, two sisters, and a legacy of 1/9 of the estate to a stranger.

The Poet As Mathematician
Teacher Page

For the problem in the student activity, the brother receives 46/144 of the estate and each sister receives 23/144 of the estate. The rest of the estate is divided between the widow, who receives 1/4, and a stranger, who receives 1/9, as stipulated in the problem (1 – 1/9 – 1/4 = 2x + x + x).

Greek mathematicians Euclid, Archimedes, and Thales are well known to any mathematics student. However, none of their writings survived to be read by modern-day European mathematicians. Islamic mathematicians were the first to translate the Greek writings, and their translations account for nearly all the information we have about ancient Greek mathematicians. Islamic mathematicians also served as a conduit between Hindu and European mathematicians. For example, they revealed to Europe the Hindu concept of zero.

Although most advancements in Islamic mathematics were in the fields of algebra and number theory, some concerned geometry. In particular, Abu'l-Wafa' (940–998) made several advancements in geometry. In *Zij al-Majisti*, he presented trigonometry tables accurate to eight decimals and also introduced the secant and cosecant functions. He is also credited with discovering the Law of Sines, and he was the first mathematician to use the tangent function.

Extension

One of Abu'l-Wafa's constructions is an alternative method for dividing a segment into congruent parts. Ask students to divide a random segment into a specific number of parts, following these directions:

1. Given segment *AB*, construct perpendicular segments in opposite directions at each endpoint.

2. Mark off two congruent segments on each perpendicular segment.

3. Draw segment *RT* to intersect segment *AB* at point *Y*.

4. Draw segment *QS* to intersect segment *AB* at point *X*.

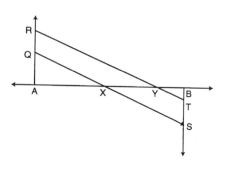

The set of construction directions above will divide a segment into three congruent parts. Segment *AB* has been divided so that *AX = XY = YB*. To divide segment *AB* into four congruent segments, mark off three congruent segments on each perpendicular segment. For five congruent segments, mark off four congruent segments on each perpendicular segment. The number of congruent segments marked off on each perpendicular segment is one less than the desired number of congruent divisions.

Receiving Credit for Another's Work

Sometimes, one mathematician has received credit for what another mathematician discovered. Venn Diagrams, named after English mathematician John Venn, were first used nearly 200 years earlier by Leonhard Euler. In turn, Euler's Formula was first discovered 100 years earlier by René Descartes. For Euler and Descartes, their reputations were not much affected, and both were well known for other mathematics. It was different for William E. Wallace (1768–1843).

Wallace made a discovery in 1787 that eventually became known as Simson's Line, after Roger Simson (1687–1768). Why was Wallace's discovery named for a dead mathematician? Simson was famous for his modern-English translation of Euclid's *Elements*. It was a very popular translation, and its appendix was continually updated with newly discovered theorems. One of the new theorems added to Simson's translation was Wallace's discovery, which became associated with Simson and, soon after, became known as Simson's Line. Although Wallace was a respected mathematician, he never achieved the fame and honors that would have come to him had his discovery been known as Wallace's Line.

For this activity, construct Simson's (Wallace's) Line by following these directions:

1. Inscribe triangle *ABC* in circle *O*.

2. Select point *Q* on circle *O*.

3. Construct segment *QX*, perpendicular to segment *AB*, segment *QY* perpendicular to segment *BC*, and segment *QZ* perpendicular to segment *AC*.

4. Draw Simson's (Wallace's) Line, the line that passes through points *X*, *Y*, and *Z*.

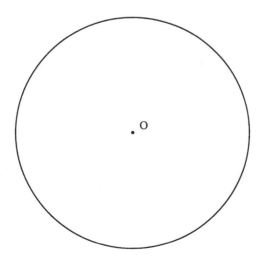

Receiving Credit for Another's Work
Teacher Page

The diagram below shows Simson's (Wallace's) Line as constructed in the student activity.

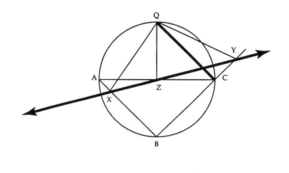

Wallace was not the only mathematician to lose fame (and possibly fortune) to others. Johann Bernoulli (1667–1748) simply sold his chance for enduring fame. French noble Marquis de L'Hopital hired Bernoulli to tutor him in calculus. L'Hopital was an amateur mathematician, and Bernoulli was one of the few mathematicians who understood the newly discovered calculus. As part of the tutoring arrangement, Bernoulli agreed not only to tutor L'Hopital, but also to "communicate all discoveries [to L'Hopital] with the request not to mention them to others."

Bernoulli did indeed make such a discovery: a rule for finding the limit of a fraction when both the numerator and the denominator approach zero. As per the agreement, Bernoulli sent word about the rule to L'Hopital and told no one else about it. L'Hopital revealed it to the world in 1696 in *Analyse des Infinitement*. The book was very popular, and Bernoulli's findings became known as L'Hopital's Rule. After L'Hopital died in 1705, Bernoulli tried to gain the credit for the rule, but his attempts were in vain. He spent the next 40 years trying to claim the fame to which he was rightfully entitled. Today, every calculus student is familiar with L'Hopital's Rule.

Extension

Another activity in this book is devoted to Fermat's Point (See "The Prince of Amateurs," p. 170), named after French mathematician Pierre de Fermat. In fact, Fermat himself never located this point. He simply proposed the problem to some of the mathematicians with whom he corresponded. Italian mathematician Evangelista Torricelli suggested the following procedure for locating Fermat's Point. Present Torricelli's procedure to students and ask them to replicate it.

---

1. Construct triangle *ABC*.

2. Construct an equilateral triangle on each side of triangle *ABC*.

3. Construct a circumscribed circle about each of the equilateral triangles.

The intersection of the three circles, point *F*, is Fermat's Point.

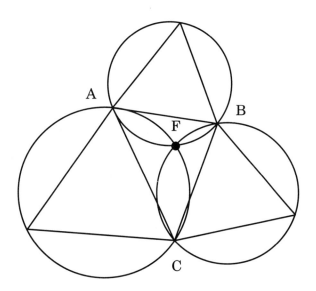

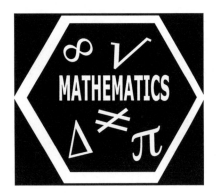

The Family Man

The professional lives of most mathematicians rarely involve their families, even though most of them marry and raise children. The life of Swiss mathematician Leonhard Euler (1707–1783) was different. He was a family man, who spent most of his time at home raising his family—and what a family it was. Euler helped his wife to raise 13 children! You might wonder how much mathematics Euler could have accomplished with so many children in the house. Actually, Euler is known for the tremendous amount of mathematics writings he produced. One estimate states that Euler produced 800 printed pages of material every year and also wrote about 4,000 letters each year, most of them to other mathematicians about mathematics. Euler is also known for popularizing the symbol π and for inventing the symbol i to represent $\sqrt{-1}$. One must wonder how Euler, with a family of 13 children, ever found the time to write about geometry, calculus, networks, number theory, graph theory, optics, and even ship design.

One of Euler's discoveries is called Euler's Line. It involves the four concurrency points of any random triangle: the incenter, circumcenter, orthocenter, and centroid. In 1765, Euler proved that three of these points are always collinear. That is, three of these points always lie on a single line.

For this activity, follow these steps to construct Euler's Line:

1. Construct the incenter, point *W*, the concurrent point of the three angle bisectors of triangle *ABC*.

2. Construct the circumcenter, point *X*, the concurrent point of the three perpendicular bisectors of the three sides of triangle *ABC*.

3. Construct the orthocenter, point *Q*, the concurrent point of the three altitudes of triangle *ABC*.

4. Construct the centroid, point *Z*, the concurrent point of the three medians of triangle *ABC*.

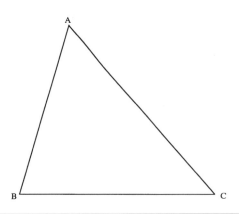

The Family Man
Teacher Page

Which three of the points constructed in the activity on the previous page are collinear? That is, which three points form Euler's Line? The three collinear concurrency points on Euler's Line are the circumcenter, the orthocenter, and the centroid.

In the eighteenth century, Swiss mathematicians produced more mathematics writings than mathematicians in either Germany, France, or England. Of course, there was but a single Swiss mathematician who was writing about mathematics at that time—Leonhard Euler. It would seem that Euler wrote about every field of mathematics during his lifetime. Some estimates of the amount of his writings suggest they would fill nearly 100 volumes! The fact that he wrote while raising 13 children, and then while blind in his later years, is all the more impressive. Euler was always on the payroll of one university or another, and this certainly helped allow him to raise such a large family and be so prolific a writer. In fact, for a number of years, Euler was supported simultaneously by more than one university. He received stipends for the last 50 years of his life. Although Euler was thus spared a routine job, one can never say that he didn't earn his keep.

As accomplished a mathematician as Euler was, he still made some errors in his mathematics. For example, he believed that 2/0 was twice as large as 1/0. It was not until a century later that Cantor proved that such expressions were impossible to order by magnitude.

Extension

If Euler's Line is drawn as a segment joining the three collinear concurrency points, it is related to the Nine-Point Circle (see "The Silver Lining," p. 172). The midpoint of Euler's Line (Segment) is also the center of the Nine-Point Circle, a fact that Euler knew. In some references, the Nine-Point Circle is erroneously called Euler's Circle, but Euler only found six of the nine points that lie on the Nine-Point Circle. Have students verify that the midpoint of Euler's Line (Segment) is also the center of the Nine-Point Circle.

The Prince of Amateurs

French mathematician Pierre de Fermat (1601–1665) is called the "Prince of Amateurs." Why such a title? Fermat never published any of his discoveries, and he never earned a penny from his mathematics. Nevertheless, he made many discoveries in mathematics and wrote about them in letters to outstanding mathematicians throughout Europe. He began the study of Probability Theory and made discoveries in geometry, calculus, and trigonometry. He is also known for Fermat's Point.

Fermat's Point is located at a minimum total distance from three other points. Fermat's Point would be a suitable location for a delivery company that wanted to locate its headquarters at a minimum distance from the three cities where it did business. The directions for finding Fermat's Point are the following:

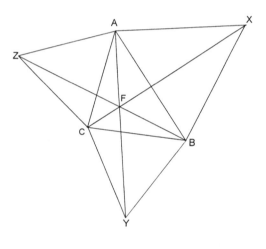

1. Draw triangle *ABC*.

2. Construct an equilateral triangle on each side of triangle *ABC*.

3. Label the new triangles *ABX*, *BCY*, and *ACZ*.

4. Draw segments *AY*, *BZ*, and *CX*.

The intersection of these three segments, point *F*, is Fermat's Point.

For this activity, use information about Fermat's Point to solve the following problem:

You have been asked to locate the hub of a new express-package delivery company, Overnight Deliveries. This company plans to deliver packages among Miami, Los Angeles, and Chicago. The packages from each city will be flown to the hub location first. Then, the packages will be delivered to the proper city. Use the map of the United States on page 33 to show where you would locate the hub so that air travel is kept to a minimum. The hub is located at Fermat's Point. When you have located the hub, label it as point *F*.

The Prince of Amateurs
Teacher Page

The location of the hub is shown on the map below. Students might be encouraged to use some practical considerations before selecting a hub site. The nearest large city to Fermat's Point, *F*, might be a suitable location because it would supply various services needed by such a hub. For this problem, St. Louis might be a hub site.

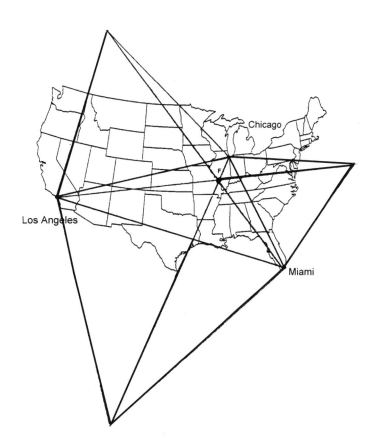

The Prince of Amateurs Teacher Page continues on page 172.

Fermat's title as Prince of the Amateurs is well deserved, but how did he earn a living and still make so many discoveries in mathematics? Fermat was a civil servant for the French government in Beaumont-le-Lomagne, a town near Toulouse in southwestern France. Because he was involved with many court cases in his local district, he was cautious not to become too friendly with any of the other citizens who lived there. Thus, Fermat spent all his spare time at home with his family, allowing him plenty of time to explore mathematics and write to other mathematicians about what he discovered. It was in such a correspondence that Fermat first proposed the minimum-distance problem that resulted in Fermat's Point. Frenicle de Bessey (1602–1675) found this solution for the location of Fermat's Point.

Extension

A point related to Fermat's Point is the circumcenter of a triangle, which is the center of a circle circumscribed about a triangle. The circumcenter is the point that is equidistant from the vertices of a triangle. Using the data from the student activity, the circumcenter would be the location of a hub that is equidistant from the three cities, rather than at a total minimum distance from the three cities. Have students locate the circumcenter for the map activity by constructing the perpendicular bisectors of the three sides of the triangle formed by cities Miami, Los Angeles, and Chicago. The bisectors meet at the circumcenter, which is located in Texas. This site would be the location of the home office for a salesperson who wants to travel the same distance from home to each of these three cities.

The Silver Lining

You have heard the saying "Behind every cloud is a silver lining." For Jean Victor Poncelet (1788–1867), it was difficult to find the silver lining in a miserable jail cell in Saratoff, Russia. How did this budding mathematician find himself in a Russian prison cell? He was captured when French troops under the command of Napoleon attacked Moscow. Poncelet spent a year in prison before he was released.

Before he joined Napoleon's army, Poncelet had been enrolled in the prestigious École Polytechnique. While there, he had an outstanding mathematics professor, Gaspard Monge (1746–1818), who taught Poncelet algebra and geometry. The mathematics lessons from Monge helped Poncelet during his imprisonment.

While in prison, Poncelet re-created all the geometry and algebra he had been taught. He literally rewrote his old textbooks and all his classwork. When he finished, he began to take his mathematics lessons even further. He developed a new way of understanding geometry, called projective geometry. In 1822, eight years after he was released from prison, Poncelet published his ideas about projective geometry in *Traite des Properties des Figures*. Eventually, the study of projective geometry became a new field of mathematics. Poncelet might have developed his ideas of projective geometry even without a year in a Russian prison, but the time he spent in a cell with nothing to do helped him clarify his thoughts. Projective geometry was the silver lining behind the cloud of a Russian prison cell.

Poncelet is also known for the Nine-Point Circle. He collaborated on this discovery with a classmate from the École Polytechnique, Charles Branchion (1785–1864). Together, they published a paper describing the Nine-Point Circle in 1820. For this activity, construct a Nine-Point Circle following these steps:

1. Construct the midpoints of the three sides of triangle *QRS*, and label the midpoints *A*, *B*, and *C*, respectively, in segments *QS*, *QR*, and *RS*.

2. Construct the altitudes from vertices *Q*, *R*, and *S*, and label their points of intersection in opposite sides *D*, *E*, and *F*, respectively.

3. Label the orthocenter (the point where the three altitudes constructed in step 3 meet) as point *O*.

4. Find the midpoints of *OQ*, *OR*, and *OS*, and label them *G*, *H*, and *I*, respectively.

5. Construct the circle that passes through these nine points: *A*, *B*, *C*, *D*, *E*, *F*, *G*, *H*, and *I*.

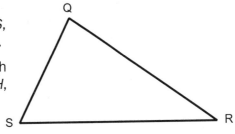

The result is the Nine-Point Circle.

The Silver Lining
Teacher Page

Student's constructions should resemble this Nine-Point Circle:

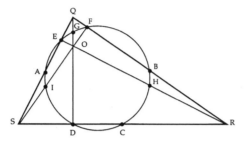

The Nine-Point Circle is also called Feurbach's Circle, for the German mathematician who independently discovered it, Karl Wilhelm Feurbach (1800–1834). Interestingly, Feurbach, too, spent time in prison. However, his experience was far different from Poncelet's. Feurbach's imprisonment occurred when he was in his early 20s and a university teacher. He became involved with some younger, radical students and was imprisoned with a group of them. Although he was quickly released, he never fully recovered from the experience.

After his release, Feurbach returned to the classroom. Although he continued to teach, Feurbach suffered a series of mental breakdowns, the last of which culminated in his threatening to disembowel any student who did not perform properly at the blackboard. After this incident, Feurbach never again returned to the classroom. He continued to decline and died young, at age 34.

Extension

Feurbach found four additional points that lie on the Nine-Point Circle. Have students add these four additional points to the Nine-Point Circle they constructed for the student activity.

1. Inscribe a circle in triangle QRS.

2. Extend the sides of triangle QRS and construct the three excircles: One excircle is tangent to side QR and rays SQ and SR; one excircle is tangent to side SR and rays QS and QR; and one excircle is tangent to side SQ and rays RS and RQ.

3. Each of these four circles is tangent to the Nine-Point Circle. Find these four new tangent points and label them J, K, L, and M.

Technically, the Nine-Point Circle is now the Thirteen-Point Circle!

Index

177

About the Author

Art Johnson is an award-winning teacher who has taught mathematics in middle school and high school since graduating from Tufts University. During that time he has won the Christa McAuliffe Sabbatical, The Presidential Award for Excellence in Mathematics Teaching, the Teacher of the Year Award for New Hampshire, the Radio Shack Award for Teaching Excellence, and was profiled by the Disney Teacher of the Year Award Program. He earned a doctorate in Mathematics Education from Boston University in 1997. Art is the author of a wide range of books, articles, and activities dealing with mathematics and mathematics education.